A WAYFARING SIN-EATER

And Other Tales
Of Appalachia

A WAYFARING SIN-EATER

And Other Tales Of Appalachia

James Gay Jones

Emeritus Professor of History
Gienville State Collage

McClain Printing Company
INCORPORATED 1958

Charleston, WV

ISBN 13: 978-0-87012-464-8

Distributed by:

West Virginia Book Company
1125 Central Ave. Charleston, WV 25302
www.wvbookco.com

Contents

Preface

It has been said that, over the centuries, Great Britain has had a greater density of ghosts than any other area of equal size in the whole world. This affinity for ghosts was brought to this country by the early settlers from the British Isles as a respected legacy of their Old Country heritage. In subsequent years, the descendants of those who settled in the isolated section of mid-Appalachia have preserved that legacy to a large extent whereas the descendants of those compatriots who settled elsewhere in this country during the era of colonization seem to have been less fortunate in that respect. While the general population over the years was being infiltrated by wave after wave of migrants with varied cultures, the hill-dwelling people lived from generation to generation in such isolation they were able to preserve their cultural heritage with little change. Moreover, they added many additional contributions of ghost stories, folk tales and ballads from their own exciting experiences and often embellished them with their vivid imaginations. From this rich source of mountain lore have come the tales presented here.

From time immemorial, people have used folk tales and ballads for the preservation of certain events in their history. So it was with the people of mid-Appalachia. Although at times illiteracy was widespread throughout the region, that did not deter them from preserving the memorable events of their past through oral repetition from one generation to another. With long memories, they transferred to their descendants the story of their past in a spoken language that had changed but little from that of the first settlers who came here. Words and expressions that had long since become archaic or obsolete elsewhere were still being used by them in their everyday conversation. Through the media of ballads and folk tales they expressed their joys as well as their frustrations. They taught, through their ghost stories, that the ghost of a person who had been murdered may seek revenge against the perpetrator of the crime. In their ballads, they sang of the ecstasy of young love, the sadness of misguided romance and the anguish and despair of misfortune. Also, they found the time to relate tall tales to help lighten the tedium of the cheerless days of their lives.

These people were reminded by the circuit riders who visited with them in their homes from time to time of the need of some formal education for their children. That would be a more effective and secure way by which their heritage could be preserved, they were told. Some parents, however, had reservations about the establishment in their midst of anything that might bring some power of regulation by outlanders. They were so protective of their way of life, they looked upon anything that appeared to be markedly different from theirs as evil and to be avoided. Therefore, those characteristics of the outlanders they frowned upon were called outlandish, a word that became firmly embedded in their everyday working language.

In order to present a truer picture of the people of this area, it should be mentioned that there were some literate families whose homes were always open to outlanders. They were interested in the activities of the world outside their region and subscribed to metropolitan newspapers such as the *Toledo Blade* and the *Cincinnati Enquirer*. Even they, however, were generally opposed to any overt attempt by outsiders to regulate their affairs.

The story of the long struggle of these hill people for a satisfactory school system is a dismal one. From the beginning, the Virginia government made no sincere effort to provide schools for the mountainous area of the western part of the state. Whenever the number of youth of school age in a community merited the opening of a school for them, the initiative to provide one was left to the parents of the youth concerned. Often a log building for a school would be erected and placed under the trusteeship of three responsible persons of the community. Their duties were to supervise the use of the building, provide for its upkeep and heating and to hire and fire the teachers. Although the illiterate condition of many of the people did not lessen their dignity nor respect for themselves and the way they lived, some wanted a better education for their children.

Because of a lack of funds, the school trustees often found it difficult to hire qualified teachers. Occasionally a teacher would be given free board and room in the homes of the parents of the pupils along with some other form of remuneration. There were times when teachers were paid in goods such as corn, potatoes, turnips, and furs. Some prospective teachers were known to go to great lengths to get a teaching position. On one occasion during an interview when a trustee inquired whether he believed the earth was flat or round, the resourceful applicant replied: "I can teach it either way."

After the state of West Virginia was formed, laws were passed for the establishment of a free public school system and for compulsory attendance of school-age children who lived within two miles of a school. Because of the deplorable means of transportation and communication at that time, little effort was made by state officials for several years to implement the legislation with any uniform enforcement procedures. Nevertheless, within a few decades what became known as common schools, or one-room rural schools, arose literally by the hundreds throughout the region.

The teachers in those schools were chiefly late teenage youth who had completed the common school course, insofar as it was a course, and had passed a written examination prepared by the county superintendent of schools. Many of those teachers looked upon teaching as a stepping stone to something better, such as a profession, which teaching was definitely not at that time. Those in authority at the state level regarded this method for the certification of teachers with little or no regard for professional training as the greatest weakness of the public school system. The charge that many teachers were certificated through "love and affection" as well as "some well placed ten dollar bills" was held to be the chief reason for the general incompetence in the school system.

As a means to try to remove some of the most glaring evils of the teacher selection system, the state legislature, in 1903, enacted a uniform examination law. It vested in the state superintendent of schools the power and duty to prepare questions, grade manuscripts and issue certificates to those who qualified. Under this new system, teacher examinations were to be held simultaneously in all the counties of the state and under the supervision of county examining boards. In order to prevent any repetition of fraud or other shenanigans of the past, examination questions were to be opened at the beginning of the testing period, then the resulting manuscripts were to be sealed in envelopes in the presence of the applicants and examiners and returned to the state superintendent's office.

Although the overall concept of the new examination system was a good one, the status of public morals in some counties did not sustain a vigorous enforcement of it. Some saw the new system as a "nefarious" one because it appeared to them to be state interference in local school affairs. As a result, in several counties both teachers and superintendents rebelled against the system. Prior to examination time, packages containing examination questions were opened and the questions circulated among prospective teacher applicants as an act of defiance of the law. So many illegal acts occurred, the state superintendent felt it necessary to call upon the prosecuting attorneys in the affected counties to investigate and prosecute the offenders. A vigorous enforcement of the law, in time, brought uniform compliance with it, yet not without its critics for many subsequent years. It was extremely difficult for some people who had held positions of "power" and "pull" under the old system to relinquish that and thenceforth be reduced to a "has been."

A majority of the teachers in these common schools up to 1900 were men. In those years, many of the youth who continued to attend the common school into their late teens and beyond because of having nothing better to do, often presented a discipline problem which only a person of rugged physique could handle. There were some women teachers at that time, however, who ably handled trying situations which earned them the respected, if unaffectionate, sobriquet of "Old Iron Pants." Many male teachers, after their marriage, continued to teach but made farming their chief occupation because their families could not survive on their teaching salary alone. Female teachers were not permitted to teach after marriage. School terms usually ran for three or four months, depending on the amount of school funds available, and the normal pay in many counties for one holding a first class certificate was twenty-five dollars a month.

Since the teachers had no tenure and held their position at the will of the majority of the trustees, they naturally tried to keep on good terms with them. If a trustee also happened to be a minister, school might be adjourned a part of each day for three or four weeks at a time so that revival services could be held in the school building. If a trustee was also the proprietor of a crossroads country store, that place of business often became the hangout of the teacher after school in the evenings and on Saturdays where, in association with traveling salesmen, he became more proficient in "profanity and general coarseness than in the tenets of his profession." If the trustees were politicians, it was wise for the teacher to become a member of the political faction with which they were affiliated. Politics and factionalism continued to be among the worst evils affecting the school system until the legal establishment, by relatively recent provision, of tenure for teachers.

In those early years, the salary of a county superintendent of schools was so inadequate he was forced to teach during the regular school term or in a summer normal session which prospective teachers were expected to attend. Apart from certification of teachers, he had no further control over them.

Some new state level provisions became effective in 1901 which brought about some changes in the status of the county superintendent in the school system. He was thenceforth forbidden to teach but was provided with a higher salary. In those counties which had fewer than fifty schools, the superintendent's annual salary was three hundred dollars. For counties having more than fifty schools, the salary scale rose to five hundred dollars annually in counties which had more than one hundred schools. Also, the superintendent was required to visit all the schools in his county at least once in each school term. For every school he failed to visit, the state superintendent of schools deducted three dollars from his salary. Since many of the schools were located in remote hollows where the roads in the wintertime were usually "ribbons of mud," it was practically impossible for the superintendent to fulfill the duty of school visitation.

Another problem faced by the superintendent, as well as by the teachers, was the truancy of school-age children. According to school records of 1896, 15 percent of the total school population of the state who were between the ages of six and sixteen were not in school. Furthermore, approximately one-third of those enrolled were absent during the school year. The superintendent placed the burden of investigation and reporting of truancy cases on the teachers. In cases where the teacher was the informant, the cost of prosecuting offenders was assessed against the teacher by justices of the peace. This practice not only reduced a teacher's much needed income but also produced considerable enmity against the teacher in the community. When teachers began to purposely neglect to report truancies, a system of truant officers was instituted soon thereafter.

Despite their inadequacies, the one-room rural schools became the focal point of the cultural activities of their respective communities. Sometimes after school in the evenings or on weekends, the people congregated there for a variety of community activities. The most prominent among those were contests in spelling, debating and oratory, box suppers or socials, and general meetings to discuss local politics or community problems. The schoolhouse often served as the community center for voting on election days. In time, some of the people became so attached to their schools as the center of their social life that when the time came for the consolidation of schools, it was a traumatic experience for them to see their local schools eliminated. They had felt comfortable in their provincial environment and were quite unprepared to meet the challenges they envisioned on a broader horizon.

Prior to the establishment of the district high schools soon after the turn of the century, practically all of the teachers in the schools in rural areas had been local residents. Because of their training and lack of any extended contact with people in the outland, they had continued to teach, generation after generation, in a dialect that was sprinkled with words and expressions that had long since become archaic or obsolete elsewhere. Also, many of the words they used in their everyday conversations were spoken with a pronunciation that was distinctly odd to outlanders who believed it was due to common ignorance on the part of the hill dwellers. Some examples of commonly used words of this nature were ahint for behind, fornent for before, muxed for messed up, chimbley for chimney, bile for boil, poke for bag or sack, pint for point, jine for join, rench for rinse, winder for window, drownded for drowned and summerset for somersault. The fact that they spoke differently from those in the outland never dawned on some of them until the new district high schools made their appearance.

Since there were few natives who could qualify to teach on the secondary level, it was necessary at the inception of the rural high schools to bring in teachers who were college graduates from the outland. As a result, there were mixed feelings held by the people in the community about the high schools. The better educated welcomed their coming while others who were less educated were not so sure that new things necessarily meant better things. Some could find little worth in a number of new subjects taught in these schools. On one occasion, when a farm boy returned home from high school and announced he was taking a course in animal husbandry, his father appeared irritated and a little embarrassed.

"Wal, that shore is a new wrinkle on my horn!" he exclaimed. "First time I ever heerd tell that bulls and buck sheep and boar hogs wuz called husbands!"

Some high school students became acutely embarrased when told by their teachers about their misuse or mispronunciation of certain words. The students blamed their parents and earlier teachers for failing to teach them correctly in that area of their education. It was difficult for them to understand why some of the teachers from the outland thought the hill people's dialect was a degenerate one and often a subject of amusement among the self-styled sophisticates.

When some of those students later entered college where they had opportunities to study English Literature more thoroughly, they found, to their relief, that many of the words they had been criticized for using by their high school teachers had also been used, with the same meaning, by such great writers as John Milton, Shakespeare, Chaucer and others. It was highly pleasing to those students when reputable scholars of the English language corroborated their findings and said the mountain dwellers should be proud that their ancestors had preserved their heritage so well.

In the process of gathering the material for this volume, care has been taken to properly identify those characters whose names have already been publicly reported elsewhere or whose consent has been obtained for inclusion here. In those stories where the use of the true names might bring embarrassment to someone or where the names have been forgotten, fictitious ones have been substituted. To all those concerned and generous-hearted souls who contributed tales through letters, long-distance telephone calls and in person, I am deeply grateful. A special acknowledgment is due my daughter, Alysia Jones Scott, for her dedicated assistance in manuscript preparation. For any errors found here, the author accepts full responsibility, yet asks the kind indulgence of his readers.

J.G.J.

Glenville, West Virginia
February 10, 1983

A Wayfaring Sin-Eater

Angus McCord stood, bronzed and tall, on the front porch of his rustic mountain home and gazed steadfastly down the narrow trail that meandered to the mountain pass road. His outward calm appearance belied the emotional strain he was experiencing inside. His daughter, Cassie, likewise worried, sat in the living room beside the window where she, too, could keep watch on the trail. After some time, she went out and tried to cheer her father up with small talk, but he could see that her worry was as great as his own. So, it ended with both of them staring down the trail together and little to talk about for fear their pent-up emotions might betray them.

Early in the morning of that day, Angus had asked his sons, Mike and Brian, to saddle the horses and ride to Montgomery, some twelve miles distant, to look for their brother, Caslar. He had left home two days before this day while under great emotional stress. It was a practice of his, when in such mental condition, to hide away in that hell-raising town on the Kanawha. It was now late in the afternoon and the sons had not yet returned.

Many times during the past three years, Angus, as well as the other members of his family, had had to suffer through the repercussions of Caslar's unpredictable behavior. His moods ranged from the heights of bravado to sheer cowardice. No matter which mood he experienced, it usually left him with bitter feelings toward himself. Angus did not want to believe it, but he could not dispel the thought that the devil must have control of his unfortunate son at times.

1

Caslar's strange behavior began at the time of his mother's death when he was thirteen years old. He and his mother, Flora, on a very cold winter night, had gone to a revival meeting at the community church. During the course of the services, the wood-burning stove was neglected and a numbing chill began to creep in on those persons seated near the walls of the meeting room. When Caslar noticed that his mother was shaking from the chill, he attempted to replenish the stove with more wood when it became evident no one else was going to do so. The church custodian, however, advised him not to put any more wood in the stove because the services would soon be over and they did not want to leave the building with a fire in the stove. Nevertheless, an hour later, the services were still going on. When Caslar saw his mother's lips turn purplish, he whispered to her that they should go home and not wait for the services to end. Flora reminded him that the preacher had warned the congregation at the beginning of his sermon that those who walked out before the services were over would most surely be claimed by the devil as they left the church. Despite her discomfort, Flora did not want to challenge the warning of the preacher.

When the services finally did come to an end, Flora and Caslar walked the two miles to their house through the snow on that biting cold night. Although he was not of much help, he tried to assist his mother whenever she faltered and helped her back on her feet when she fell down. As for himself, he was so cold it felt as if he were walking on someone else's legs; he knew it was just as bad, if not worse, for his mother. The following morning, Flora was not able to get out of bed and before the week had come to an end, she was dead of pneumonia.

Caslar had always been very close to his mother and it was probably true she had felt closer to him because he was the youngest child. Now that she had gone so suddenly, it was devastating for him. While all the other members of the family were shedding tears of sorrow, Caslar was shedding tears of anger. He could not understand why people accepted death with such a futile attitude. Surely, he thought, someone should decide where retribution was due. With reckless abandon, he became angry at the church custodian, at the minister and at God for having such callous-hearted people representing Him.

One night a few weeks after Flora died, Caslar quietly got out of bed on the ruse of going out of the house to relieve himself but instead, went to the church and set it on fire. When he returned to bed, his brother, Brian, with whom he slept, woke up and wondered to himself why Caslar was cold and chilling. Later, when he heard that the church building had burned to the ground, he suspected Caslar had done it but never revealed his suspicion to anyone. It was easily recognized that the manner of his mother's death had transformed him into a different person. Subsequently, there was no knowing what his reaction would be to any incident that overly distressed him.

The most recent episode that had upset Caslar and caused him to leave home occurred a couple of days before while Angus and his sons were in the woods getting some logs ready to float down river to a sawmill when the spring thaw came. Mike, the eldest of the McCord boys, was in charge of the two yoke of oxen that were snaking out the logs that day. As one log was being snaked out, it overturned a boulder under which was a nest of rattlesnakes. The oxen, on getting scent of the disturbed reptiles and hearing their ominous rattle, got out of control and stampeded. Mike, in his effort to try to halt the oxen, was maneuvered, against his better judgment, into a position below the rapidly moving log. When he tripped and fell, luckily for him, the log bounced over him, rolled down a steep embankment and pulled the oxen, in disarray, after it.

3

Even though Mike nor the oxen sustained any injuries, Caslar's witnessing of the incident was traumatic for him. He became hysterical and ran off toward home. On his arrival at the house, Cassie saw at once that he was distraught and tried to find out, in a calm and reassuring manner, what his problem was. Her inquiry only intensified his distress. When she saw him take a rifle down from a rack on the wall, her acute fright over what he might do, suddenly made her ill. Despite her nausea, she followed him, at a respectable distance, into the woods where the logging incident had occurred.

On Caslar's return, he vowed he was going to shoot the oxen for trying to kill Mike. With deft maneuvering, Angus was able to get the gun away from him; then putting an arm around his son's shoulders, he soothingly talked him into calming down. Meanwhile, Mike and Brian had gotten the oxen out of their entanglement and back on their feet again. After hobbling them securely, the two brothers set about the task of killing as many rattlesnakes as they could find by clubbing them to death. From an unseen vantage point, Cassie observed the outcome of Caslar's foolish escapade and returned to the house relieved, but still shaken over what might have taken place.

The following day, Caslar saddled his pony and rode off down the trail to the mountain pass road without saying where he was going. On the basis of past experience, it was everyone's guess he was going down to Montgomery. So now, two days later, Angus could only stare down the trail and pray that God would help to bring him safely home again.

At length, in the darkening twilight, Angus saw his sons riding up the trail, all three of them, and even at that distance, he could tell, from the manner Caslar was being helped by his brothers, that he was drunk. He had been found, Angus was informed, at the Honkatonk, one of the notorious saloons located on Montgomery's Front Street.

He was put to bed and treated by all with empathy and compassion.

Many times Angus McCord regretted his decision to raise his family here in these hills. From the very beginning, he had had some doubts about it, but had hoped he could resolve them through hard work and good management. In looking back, he could see there had always been plenty of hard work, but the management had often gone awry by events he was unable to control.

When the C&O Railroad was extended from Covington through the Allegheny Mountains into the Kanawha Valley in the early 1870s, Angus had helped to build that section of it. However, by the time the railroad had reached the falls of the Kanawha River, he had had enough of railroad building. Some areas of their work, especially through the New River Gorge, had been extremely hazardous and frightening at times. Although he did not know it at the time, he had worked through the most difficult part of the entire C&O line from its eastern terminal westward to the Ohio River.

On his return to Covington, he could not forget the vast virgin forests he had seen in the area near the junction of the New and Gauley rivers. He believed there was a great fortune awaiting someone at that place, now that the railroad had been extended through there.

Soon after his marriage to Flora Caslar, Angus returned to the Gauley River Valley where he secured title to five hundred acres of virgin timber land. His acreage was located back of some initial cutting that had been done near the mouth of the Gauley. Then with the help of others, he built a comfortable log dwelling house on an expansive level shelf on a mountainside near the trail that crossed westward out of the valley. Shortly thereafter, Angus returned to Covington and brought back his young bride to their isolated mountain home. Now, twenty-five years later and without a wife to sustain and encourage him, he was

5

still struggling for that elusive fortune that he had earlier dreamed about but, so far, had little to show for his efforts.

Angus's lack of control over Caslar was a major contributing factor to the despair that prevailed in the Mc-Cord home. Although his sons, Mike and Brian, and daughter, Cassie, had always been supportive, the unpredictability of Caslar adversely affected everyone. Since he was the youngest child in the family, all of them, especially after Flora died, felt a degree of responsibility in caring for him. On his part, Caslar showed little appreciation for what was done for him and assumed little responsibility in the activities in the timber business on the Mc-Cord estate.

There were times, when pressure began to build up in him, that Caslar would saddle his pony and ride down into the valley and stay with the Ezra Tabor family on their farm where he could be with their son, John. For several days at a time he would willingly work in the fields with the Tabors without any expectation of being paid for his work. He felt more at ease while away from home, but his greatest reward came in the evenings after work. At that time Caslar and John would saddle their ponies and go for a ride on the country road that passed nearby. Once out of sight of the Tabor house, they would urge their ponies to a gallop in a racing contest.

Also, at other times, they engaged in a variety of acrobatic activities while running at full speed. One such prank was to jump from their saddle to the bank alongside the roadway while still holding on to the pommel of the saddle and then bounce back into the saddle again all the while without any slackening of speed. One particularly hazardous trick they liked to perform was for each, while going at full speed, to switch from one horse to the other simultaneously. Oftentimes, when they returned from their riding sport, the ponies would be covered with sweat and lather while bloody foam dripped from their cut and bleeding mouths. When such activities came to Ezra's attention, he suggested that Caslar should return to his own home.

Ezra's manner of handling the situation permitted Caslar to leave in good grace and with an invitation that he would always be welcome to return. When he arrived home, he fully explained what had happened while he was visiting with the Tabor family and showed no animosity toward them. The members of his family were surprised at his new attitude and hoped it meant a turning point in his life.

During the fall and early winter months, Caslar remained home and took an active part in the work about the farm. Angus was so pleased with the change in his son's attitude, he bought a pair of knee-high leather boots for each of his sons. Caslar's response was to put his boots on and walk to the Tabor home to show them to John despite the blustery weather and a temperature that was below freezing.

On Caslar's arrival at the Tabor home, he took off his boots and warmed his feet before the fire in the open fireplace. As he did so, John put on the boots and laced them up to see how they felt on him. At that moment, Ezra entered the house and reported that one of the horses had a severe case of colic and asked John to go to a neighbor's house for help. Momentarily forgetting that he still had Caslar's boots on, John quickly put on a heavy coat and toboggan and hurried out into the worsening weather. Thinking he might be of some help, Caslar put on John's shoes and went with Ezra to the barn to keep watch on the ill horse.

On their arrival at the barn, they found the horse in great pain and was kicking and prancing about its stall in such manner it was unwise for anyone to venture in. So, after a number of attempts, they were able, from a safe place in the manger, to get a rope lasso around its neck and secure it to a manger post.

When John returned with two men from a neighboring farm, one of the men had a quart of home-brewed whiskey which he claimed would relieve the horse of its gas pains. Thereupon, the men pried open its mouth and emptied the contents of the bottle down its throat.

The reaction of the horse was a most violent one. With a loud cry of pain, it spread-eagled its legs and fell to the floor of the stall with a resounding thump which forced an emission of sharp bursts of air from both ends of the tightly swollen animal. Within moments, it was back on its feet again and with a few well-placed kicks, it knocked down the rear wall of the stable. Then with a powerful tug, it broke loose from the rope noose and ran out of the barn.

The men followed into the bone-chilling night air completely at a loss to know what to do next. From where they stood, they could clearly hear the beat of the horse's hooves striking the frozen ground as it raced up the country road. Next came the easily recognizable sound of its spread-eagle fall on the roadway and followed by a chilling cry of excruciating pain. Soon they heard it running again, the clippety-clop of its galloping gradually growing fainter as it raced farther into the night.

Meanwhile, John had saddled another horse and hurriedly rode off after the distraught one. Not knowing what else to do, the men returned to the shelter of the barn. They did not believe John had the slightest chance of recovering the drunken and pain-crazed horse. In its mad flight, they believed, it would either kill itself or become so severely maimed it would have to be destroyed.

After waiting at the barn for a time, Ezra and the neighbor man decided to go out and help in the search for the horse while Caslar returned to the Tabor house to wait. Hours later, the men came back, chilled to the bone, and reported they had seen neither John nor the horses. They had walked several miles up and down the country road and checked among livestock on neighboring farms in the vicinity of the road, all to no avail.

Sometime later, while the men sat at the fireplace warming themselves, they heard the whinny of a horse. They ran outside and found that both horses had returned but John was nowhere to be seen. Ezra instructed that the ill horse be stabled in the barn, then he mounted the saddled horse and rode off to look for John. The others returned to the house to replenish their lanterns with oil after which they, too, joined in the search.

Shortly after daybreak the next morning, John's body was found in a brush-choked ravine below the roadway about two miles from the Tabor homeplace. It appeared that he had been kicked or struck on the head, knocked unconscious and fallen into the ravine. While in that condition, he had frozen to death.

John's body was returned to the Tabor home to be prepared for burial. Because of the frozen condition of the body, it was decided that the clothes, including Caslar's new boots, would have to be cut off. Caslar's reaction to the prospect of seeing his boots ruined was frightening. He flew into a rage and in a ranting tirade, berated all those present and said he hoped John's soul would go to Hell. It took two strong men to get Caslar out of the house. After taking off John's shoes which he had been wearing, he walked barefoot over the frozen ground to his house.

Subsequently, at the Tabor home, a consultation of great import was held by the family and close relatives. They were very much disturbed over the curse Caslar had put on John's soul. After a lengthy discussion, it was decided that the ritual of the laying on of hands would be observed. Also, it was decided that, under no circumstances, would Caslar be permitted to attend the funeral. They did not consider the probability that he might not want to attend; they wanted to be certain he would have no choice.

So, on the day of the funeral, as John's draped body was being carried on a litter from the Tabor house to the cemetery, members of the family and other well-wishing relatives and friends placed their hands on the body and prayed short prayers, some silently, some audible, for his deliverance from Caslar's curse.

For several days after Caslar returned home and, while nursing his swollen feet, he was despondent and uncommunicative. The other members of the family became so concerned about his condition that his grandmother, Kate McCord, who lived in Covington, was informed about him and urged to come and try to cheer him up. A few days later, Kate, robust and genial, arrived and brought along a new pair of leather boots for Caslar and a young Scotch terrier for the family. Both gifts seemed to have been well-chosen for, like magic, they soon brought the entire household back to normal again. When the time came that Caslar could walk without any pain, he insisted that he join the other men-folk to help them cut more logs in preparation for the spring thaw.

The spring thaw normally brought a considerable rise in the Gauley River down which the logs the McCords cut would be floated to a sawmill a couple of miles downstream. Since coming to this location, Angus had seen a most remarkable change take place in the manner of sawing lumber. The method used here on his arrival was the water-powered sawmill. It was a slow process that required an abundance of patience from everyone concerned in its operation. The swing of the long-bladed saw was so slow that lumbermen called it the "up today and down tomorrow" mill. The new mill that replaced it was steam-powered and much more efficient in operation and tremendously more productive in output. At the point of the mill's location on the riverbank the river would be filled with logs when the sawmill was in operation; long iron chains hauled the logs, one at a time, up inclined planes, to meet the saws which swiftly turned them into lumber.

During January and February of 1902, the weather was extremely cold in the Gauley River Valley. Temperatures were much below freezing and hovered around zero for days at a time. Ice on the river froze to a thickness of two feet in many places. Where the river was shallow, the water froze all the way to the river bottom and in chopping out blocks of ice at those locations, live fish could be found entrapped in the ice.

Later in the spring when the Big Thaw came, the river played havoc through long stretches in the valley. The noise from the heaving and cracking in the breakup of the ice sounded like fireworks. When the high water finally receded, the banks on both sides of the river were strewn with huge blocks of ice that remained there for weeks before finally melting.

Among the blocks of ice and other debris left on the riverbank were some of the McCord logs which had been too near the flooding waters. When the weather became tolerable, Angus and his sons spent several days working to recover as many of those logs as possible. During that time, Caslar brought the terrier along with him because he had become quite attached to it. Although Angus had his doubts about the prudence of its being there, he made no mention of it out of respect for Caslar's wishes. While the men worked, the little dog ran about here and there in a vigorous, exploratory adventure. Caslar occasionally stopped working to check on the whereabouts of the terrier to see that it did not get in the way of the workers or become endangered by the shifting of the logs.

Once when Caslar looked about for the dog, he could not see it anywhere. He continued looking all around the

place and shortly he saw it jump up on a log a considerable distance away. As he stood looking at it, he was
shocked to see a bald eagle swoop down on the unsuspec-
ting dog, clutch it in its sharp talons and fly away with it
toward the wooded mountainside. The yelp of the dog
drew the attention of all the men working there and they
immediately screamed and shouted as a means to try to
scare the eagle to make it drop its prey. However, their
cries went for naught and the little dog was soon carried
out of sight into the forest.

While all stood aghast at the sight, Angus was more
concerned over what Caslar's reaction would be. He believed that Mike and Brian would see it as a circum-
stance about which they could do nothing, whereas
Caslar was unpredictable, yet most likely would find a
way to blame himself for it. On coming out of his
stunned condition, Caslar began to jump up and down
and to shake his fists in the direction the eagle had
flown, all the while cursing and screaming. Among other
things, he screamed he could not understand why he was
so bedeviled. As he ended his tirade, he said he might as
well go down to Montgomery where there were so many
other bedeviled people and be with his kind. Thereupon,
he strode away, leaving his father and brothers standing
there in an awkward silence. Before Caslar had gone very
far, Angus called to him to come back, but he acted as if
he had not heard his father and continued on his way.

The railroad town of Montgomery was located about a
dozen miles downstream from the McCord homestead. It
arose there soon after the C&O Railroad was built
through the Kanawha Valley in 1873. In the beginning it
was only a depot for the unloading of coal which was
mined on a hillside above the depot and brought in on
the Coal Valley Coal Company Railroad. When more
mines were opened up Morris Creek and east of the
depot at Crescent, an influx of people came in to work

in the mines. As a result, a town of shanties, houses, saloons, and other places of business sprang up around the depot and, in time, became known as Montgomery.

When the miners from the isolated coal camps began to flock in to town to seek supplies and entertainment, a number of additional businesses came into being as a means to supply their needs. Along Front Street, which ran alongside the railroad tracks and was the main street of town, there were a variety of business places usually found in a frontier city. The more respectable homes were located on the back streets, yet, nevertheless, had to suffer the hell-roaring reputation that Front Street gave to the town.

The most patronized businesses on Front Street were the numerous saloons among which were the Red Onion, Dalton, Honkatonk, Mecca, Tomahawk and Mammoth Cave. Although many decent and reputable people came to town because it was the main trading place in the area for miners and their families, it was also the chief attraction for all the wild and desperate characters that were to be found on every bustling frontier. Practically all men there, at that time, carried handguns and knives for real or imagined protection and, as a result, shooting and cutting scrapes occurred almost daily. Heated arguments and fistfights were so common as to attract little attention until they developed into something more lethal.

There were times when the municipal officials allowed extensive gambling, not only on Front Street, but on other streets in town as well. A variety of gambling devices, including the Big Six, penny pitches and other games of chance, ingeniously devised to easily separate money from hard-working people, could be found there. In upstairs rooms and in basements of buildings along Front Street, poker was played while across the railroad tracks the blacks played crap games.

13

For those who preferred other forms of entertainment, there was a Grand Opera house, a huge building situated near the depot. Its expansive stage, lighted by oil lamps, was the setting for melodramas like Uncle Tom's Cabin and others common to that time. In the basement of this opera house was a rathskeller, better known as "The Bear Wallow," where a variety of refreshments were available to the patrons between acts on the stage.

The open and easy flow of money in this gambling town gave Albert Vires, an unscrupulous and crafty resident of Montgomery, an idea. He hired a number of local villains, both white and black, for the express purpose of robbery. Lucky winners at the gambling devices were spied on and later waylaid and robbed. When it became necessary to kill anyone, the victim would be taken out on the C&O bridge that crossed Morris Creek and there knocked off. The bodies were then taken to an abandoned coal mine on the hill opposite town and hidden. When Vires and his henchmen were finally apprehended and the abandoned coal mine inspected, it was said that their victims found there were stacked up like cordwood. Vires was taken to the county seat at Fayetteville and held for trial. After a speedy trial, he was found guilty and hanged.

As Caslar walked toward Montgomery, his thoughts were centered largely on his inability to control the events of his life. He finally concluded that if he could not face up to the troubles that often beset him, he could get drunk and, at least temporarily, forget them. So, on his arrival in that lively and boisterous town, he went directly to the nearest saloon. Before the night was over, he was involved in a drunken brawl and, along with others, was taken to jail.

On the following day the proprietress of a local boarding house was brought to the jail for the purpose of trying to identify a person incarcerated there on a charge of mayhem who had refused to divulge his name. In a drunken brawl he had bitten off an earlobe and the end of the nose of an adversary before being brought under control. It was believed he had recently lived at the boardinghouse and the likelihood that the proprietress of that establishment would remember him, if he had, was a lead worth pursuing. It so happened that the unidentified prisoner was a cellmate of Caslar's.

The tall and robust proprietress, who also was an aggressive proponent of the temperance and anti-saloon movement at that time, welcomed the opportunity to visit the jail. On her arrival at the cell door, she not only quickly identified the prisoner but proceeded to lecture him and Caslar on the evils associated with whiskey. Even though her descriptions of the suffering imposed on the wives and children of drunkards were vivid and shocking, they made no outward impression on the prisoners. They sat on their bunks impassively without any appearance of listening. Yet the warmth and motherly attitude of the proprietress reminded Caslar of his own mother and he wondered how she might feel, if she were living, about his being in jail.

When Caslar was released from jail, he felt he had had enough of the fast living in Montgomery and immediately started back toward home. On his arrival there, he was greeted with the usual cordial reception and no questions were asked of him about his trip to the city. From his wan appearance, they could tell he had not had a happy visit so they avoided any mention of it in his presence. Luckily for all, there soon came a pleasant diversion shortly thereafter in the appearance of a stranger at the front door. Angus greeted the man and, on being informed that he wished to stay there overnight, he was invited in.

Although the McCord residence was not within sight of the mountain pass road, some travelers knew of the place either because they had been there before or they had heard it spoken of as a desirable place for overnight lodging. Because of their somewhat isolated location, the McCord family welcomed the arrival of travelers with warmth because they usually brought interesting conversation and news from the outland.

After a sumptuous supper, the family and their guest gathered around the living room fireplace and spent the evening in a spirited conversation. It soon became evident that the visitor was a person who had traveled extensively and could relate his experiences in a most interesting manner. Brian and Caslar were particularly fascinated in his tales about wolves. He mentioned that he recently talked with a man who lived a few miles north of Hodam Mountain who said he had seen a small pack of wolves, perhaps half a dozen, near his farm only a few days before. Angus then added that Bill Connelley, who lived only a few miles to the north, told him he had heard wolves howling one dark night in the woods between Buffalo Creek and Gauley River. Although conceding that there were very few wolves around any more, the visitor went to great length to tell of some frightening experiences of his grandfather's time when large packs of wolves roamed the woods at will.

The wolves were so numerous and destructive, the visitor related, that the state of Virginia, which extended westward to the Ohio River at that time, offered to pay a bounty for wolves' scalps. The amount of the bounty varied from time to time but usually was around six to eight dollars for each scalp. This induced some people to build wolf pens as a means to cash in on the bounty program in a more lucrative way. A more common method used in catching wolves was to go into the woods with a rifle and shoot them. As wolves became scarcer, some people kept wolves in enclosures and raised the whelps that were born in captivity to full development then killed them and sold their scalps for bounty payments.

Late one evening, the visitor related, his grandfather went out into the woods in hopes of getting a wolf or two for bounty payment. He had not gone far when he found fresh wolf sign. With a view of decoying a wolf within rifle shot, he uttered a howl as much like that of a wolf's as he could make it. Within seconds there came an answering cry from the dark woods. Soon this was, in turn, answered, at close intervals, from a number of locations in the forest. Now pleased with his skill as an imitator, he again made the cry and immediately there came answering howls from all sides at closer proximity. Each time he made the cry, the howls from the forest became more numerous and closer to him.

When his grandfather heard the patter of running feet among the dry leaves on all sides of him, he suddenly realized the stark danger he faced. He quickly dropped his rifle and with a surge of strength he did not realize he had, he hastily sprang to the limb of a beach tree and pulled himself to safety. No sooner had he arrived at his safe perch than the ground under the tree was overrun by a pack of snarling, hungry wolves. More and more wolves kept coming until there must have been at least a hundred of them. Now made fearless by their numbers, some leaped up against the trunk of the tree while others snarled and fought among themselves. The helpless man could only sit there, hour after hour, and watch, from the safety of his perch, his swarming tormentors with their deadly fangs flashing through froth-covered jaws. Throughout the night the ordeal continued. At daybreak the wolves began to trot away, a few at a time, until all of them had slunk back to the fastness of the forest. The visitor concluded the story by saying that his grandfather, after seeing such great potential wealth in wolves's scalps so near at hand, was more than willing to forgo that in preference to the keeping of his own scalp.

For several days after the visitor at the McCord home

17

had gone on his way, Caslar was intrigued about the catching of wolves in pens. He talked it over with Brian and asked his assistance in building a pen. Brian had his doubts about such an undertaking, one reason being the scarcity of wolves in the region at that time and the probability that bounty payments were not available; another was the fact that neither of them had ever seen a wolf pen. Caslar contended, however, that from the remarks made by the visitor in their home, he had a fairly good idea how one should be built. In view of the expected excitement from the sport, Brian finally agreed to help in the project.

After a number of hours of laborious planning and effort the brothers had a workable wolf pen completed. The pen was constructed of small poles, was six feet in length, three feet wide and four feet in height. At one end of the pen a thin board slightly wider than the pen was installed to serve as a vertical sliding trapdoor. This board was held in place by two stakes driven into the ground in front of it. Midway at the top of the trapdoor a string was attached which passed over the adjacent top end pole and inside to some bait which was located near the rear of the cage. A disturbance of the bait would release the string and permit the trapdoor to fall and close the cage. After trying it out a few times and finding it worked satisfactorily, the brothers were quite proud of their work. They then returned home to await results of their project.

On the following day, Brian and Caslar returned to the wolf pen and, on looking inside, saw they had caught a small black bear cub. They reasoned that it, through curiosity, had carelessly walked in. While debating what to do with their catch, they were suddenly surprised to see a large black bear come loping down the hill toward them. With a cry of fright, Caslar took off as fast as he could run toward home without ever looking back. On his arrival there, he burst into the house screaming that Brian was being attacked by a huge bear. Since Cassie was the only person at the house at the time, he became hysterical and cried that Brian would most surely be killed. Cassie tried to calm him down and suggested that they both go back to help Brian. Caslar, however, refused to leave the house so Cassie got a rifle and hurried out toward the location of the wolf pen. On the way there she hoped and prayed that Caslar had overacted again as he so often did.

When Cassie approached the area of the wolf pen, she saw neither Brian nor a bear. Then she heard Brian cry out to her not to come any closer but to hurry back to the house. Before taking her brother's advice, she wanted to be sure he was in a safe place and began to look around to see where he was. At the moment she spotted him high up in the forks of a tree, there came an ominous growl from behind her. Suddenly the big bear pounced upon her and, at the same time, knocked the rifle she carried, several feet away. While the bear mauled Cassie, Brian hurried down from the branches of the tree and, without thinking of his own safety, rushed to the aid of his sister. He quickly snatched the rifle up and with great care not to harm Cassie, took deliberate aim and fired. With a roar of pain, the bear rose up on its rear legs then fell over dead. Cassie, scratched and bleeding, lay moaning and in a state of shock. As Brian looked down on the crumpled body of his sister, the extent of her sacrifice to help him suddenly overwhelmed him. Then with a flow of strength he did not realize he had, Brian gently lifted his sister in his arms and hurried with her back to the house.

By the time they arrived there, Angus and Mike had returned home. When Angus saw Cassie's serious condition, he directed Mike to saddle a horse and go after a doctor. Within moments, Mike was galloping down the trail toward the pass road. Meanwhile, Cassie had been put to bed and Angus and Brian were trying to make her as comfortable as they knew how. Caslar, ashen-faced and uncommunicative, nervously paced about from room to room like a zombie.

When the doctor came, he dressed Cassie's wounds and after examining her thoroughly, reported that as far as he could determine, there were no bones broken. Although she had partially recovered from shock, the doctor advised that it would be wise to keep a close watch over her for several hours just in case she might have a relapse. As the doctor left, Angus walked with him out to the front porch and there they conversed for some time in voices inaudible to the other members of the family. When Angus returned inside, he went to Cassie's bedside, sat down in a chair and, after briefly looking at his daughter, he covered his face with his hands.

While Mike took care of the outdoor chores, Brian set about fixing some supper for the family. No one asked Caslar to help with anything nor did he volunteer to help. He continued his restless walking as if in a trance. At length he stopped at the open door to Cassie's bedroom and looked in. He saw his father still sitting there with his face buried in his hands and on the bed he could see his sister with her face covered with bandages and as still as death. As he looked upon the scene, a feeling of guilt and remorse swept over him. He wondered what his father and the doctor had talked about while they were on the front porch. Was Cassie going to die? As he continued to view the sad sight, he wondered what his father might be thinking. Never before had he seen the powerful frame of his father look so slumped and dejected as he was at that moment. Was it his own fault that Cassie was in this condition? Why was it that he so often brought pain and anguish to others? Did the devil really take control of his destiny when he burned the church building down? More and more questions he put to himself but could find no solid answers. Then with his eyes glistening with tears, Caslar went out of the house and resumed his walking without any idea where it might take him.

Down the trail Caslar went and, on reaching the pass road, he turned right onto it and continued down into the valley. He felt he should get away from his family in order not to bring any more grief or hardship to them. On and on into the deepening twilight he trudged without any thought of his destination. Nor did he realize that he seemingly was being drawn, by a force he could not control, toward the infamous town of Montgomery.

For several days after arriving in Montgomery, Caslar bummed about town while trying to forget the mistakes he had made in the past. Despite his efforts to get lost in the faceless crowd, he ended up in a saloon brawl following a disputed card game in which he was seriously injured when a constable pistol-whipped him. While he still lay semiconscious on the floor, a city policeman appeared on the scene. When he saw what the constable had done, he attempted to arrest him. The response of the constable was to draw his gun, whereupon the policeman shot him dead and his body fell heavily on the floor across Caslar. As soon as the turmoil had quieted down, Caslar was carried out and taken to the city jail.

While he languished there, he was unaware of the events that his brawl and subsequent beating had precipitated in town. The brothers and other close relatives of the slain constable came to seek vengeance and for hours they terrorized the town. The policeman who had shot the constable was spirited away to an undisclosed place of safety. In the meantime, word was sent to the county seat at Fayetteville for the sheriff, Nehemiah Daniels, to come and restore order.

21

In due time, Sheriff Daniels, with a heavily armed posse, arrived in Montgomery. As they stepped down from the special train that brought them there, they saw one of the desperadoes standing on a street corner opposite the depot. With a naturally brave disposition and the added strength of his official position backing him, Daniels walked across the street to where the wanted man stood. Gently touching the man on the shoulder, the sheriff said: "You are under arrest!" With lightning speed, the man drew his gun and shot the sheriff through the heart. As Daniels fell dead in the street, relatives of the killer came out from all directions with guns drawn and, in defiance of the posse, ran toward the hillside where they barricaded themselves in an abandoned coal mine.

Hours later, the desperadoes surrendered when Mayor Tom Davies and Police Chief Parry promised them protection from a mob that had begun to congregate nearby and threaten them with annihilation. When darkness came, all of the men in the abandoned mine were permitted to steal away, one at a time, into the night except the one who had shot the sheriff. That man was surrounded by the posse and hurried to a waiting train at the depot and from there was immediately taken to the county jail at Fayetteville to await trial for murder.

Back at the McCord homestead, Cassie was recovering satisfactorily from her wounds. Soon after she was attacked by the bear, her grandmother, Kate, had been informed of it, but because of a minor illness of her own at the time, was not able to come over from Covington for a few days. On her arrival at her son's house, she brought a commanding presence that could not be ignored. When she learned that Caslar had been absent from home for several days, she confronted Angus about it.

"Why haven't you sent someone to find Caslar?" she queried him.

"Caslar is no longer a boy, Mother," Angus replied. "He is of age and I don't have the power to make him stay here, or to do anything, for that matter. I'm sure you know as well as the rest of us here that he has not been himself much of the time since his mother died. Oftentimes, he seems to be under sinister alien power and completely beyond our help."

"That's the more reason why we must try harder to help him," Kate responded. "Do you have any idea where he might be?"

"My guess would be that he's down at Montgomery," Angus replied.

"If he is, someone must get him out of that Gomorrah on the Kanawha!" she vehemently cried. Then turning to Mike, she ordered him to go to Montgomery and look for Caslar.

Mike at once went to the barn and saddled two horses, one for himself and one for Caslar, and rode off down the trail. After traveling a couple of miles or so, he met a man who stopped and inquired if he knew where Angus McCord lived. When Mike informed him that he was a son of the person he sought, the man said he brought some sad news for the family. Thereupon, in a manner as gentle and compassionate as he could muster, the man stated that Caslar was dead; he had choked himself to death with his own shoelaces while in the city jail in Montgomery. His body was still at the jail waiting for his family to take it away.

With a heavy heart, Mike turned around and went back home to report the shocking news to the family. In the midst of the grieving that ensued, Kate emerged as the strong one of the family who would supervise the making of the final arrangements for Caslar's funeral and burial. A family conference was called for the announcement of the assignments to be carried out.

"We are faced with a very serious situation," Kate

23

began. "Caslar has been feeding on the forces of evil in that sin-ridden city of Montgomery. His soul is in jeopardy and we've got to try to save it. His self-destruction is a most serious offense in the eyes of God. There is nothing we can do now to save his body, but we can at least make a final effort to save his soul. We will have to get a sin-eater to relieve him of having to bear such a heavy burden of sin into purgatory. We all need to know that this ritual is to be a central part of our final preparations for Caslar. Around this, the other things we need to do will rightly fall into place."

When the family conference ended, the family members began at once to carry out their assigned duties. Angus and Brian set out to Montgomery to get Caslar's body. While at Montgomery, Angus was to send word on to Maggie Doone at White Sulphur Springs, who was knowledgeable of the ritual of sin-eating as practiced in earlier times in the Old Country, to come immediately to the McCord home.

Mike's assignment was a more exacting one. Kate explained to him that he was to go to the pass road and wait for the appearance of a wayfaring stranger. To qualify for sin-eating, such a person would have to be someone who was not acquainted with the McCord family; moreover, he must not tarry in the community after the ritual was concluded.

"We have to be honest with the sin-eater," Kate explained to Mike. "In no way must we try to deceive him. If we did, it would bring grief to us all. On the other hand, the sin-eater must be sincere in his agreement with us. If he accepts with deception or greed in mind, then the Lord have mercy on his soul! If you think the stranger qualifies, and he is walking, promise him a horse for his help," Kate continued. "If he accepts, we'll let him have Caslar's pony. If he already has a horse, promise him a rifle. If he doesn't understand what is ex-

24

pected of him, tell him that will be explained to him later on. Don't ask the one you choose what his name is; it's best that he be remembered only as a wayfaring stranger."

For hours Mike tarried at the pass road without any success. The few persons who passed were residents of the community and in talking with them, he was thankful they did not ask him why he was waiting there. He was sure he would not have told them he was waiting for a sin-eater. That was someone he had never heard of until his grandmother brought it up, and he was not prepared to explain something he did not understand. While there, he saw his father and Brian return with Caslar's body. After they turned off the pass road to go up the trail to the house, he became so saddened he broke down and cried and went behind some bushes to hide until he got control of himself again. When dusk came, he returned to the house to be at his brother's wake.

Early the following morning, Mike resumed his vigil beside the pass road. He hoped someone would come along soon for this was an assignment that was not particularly to his liking. One of his worries was that he might choose someone who would not be acceptable to his grandmother; another was that he might not find anyone at all.

About noon Mike saw a person riding a horse up the pass road toward him. As the rider came closer, he observed that it was a middle-aged woman dressed in black clothes. He quickly ran over in his mind what his grandmother had told him about the kind of person to be chosen for sin-eating and could not recall that the sin-eater had to be a man. Still, he was uncertain what he should do. His anxiety in that regard, however, was short-lived. When the woman rode within speaking distance, she inquired of him how to get to the McCord residence and he rightly guessed she was Maggie Doone, the person his grandmother had sent for. She thanked Mike for his help in directing her and, without another word, rode up the trail toward the McCord house.

About mid-afternoon a young man came walking up the pass road. When he came up to where Mike was sitting on a log beside the road, he stopped to rest for a spell. In the ensuing conversation, the stranger related that he was on his way to visit an uncle who operated a lumber business in the upper area of the Elk River Valley. When Mike pointed out to him that he could have gone by train nearly all the way to his destination if he had taken the train to Charleston, then up the Elk Valley, the stranger replied:

"Yes, I know! That was my plan and I had paid my train fare to Charleston; but old stupid me had to stop in Montgomery and there I lost all my money in a crooked poker game. There was no use for me to go on to Charleston without any money for train fare beyond there so I decided to try my luck by walking over the mountain. I'm not so sure it was such a good idea if the rest of the way is like what I've already covered."

The stranger also related that he was a veteran of the Spanish-American War, had tried a number of trades and odd jobs without much success and had recently served a hitch in the navy, getting his discharge at Norfolk only a few days before coming here. He said he was now on his way to see what living in a lumber camp in the mountains was like.

Now that the opportunity Mike had looked for was at hand, he felt it much too awkward to ask the traveler to serve as sin-eater. Instead, he invited him to stay at the McCord home overnight. When the man accepted the invitation, a burden seemed to be lifted from Mike's shoulders. He decided to let his grandmother have an opportunity to appraise him; if she liked what she saw, she could personally explain the situation to him.

Soon after Mike's arrival at the house with his guest, he was told that his grandmother wanted to see him in the kitchen.

"Did the stranger agree to help us?" Kate inquired of Mike in a low voice.

"I didn't ask him," Mike replied. "Since he agreed to stay overnight with us, I thought it would be better if someone who knows more about sin-eating would ask him. I might have scared him away."

"Perhaps you did what is best," Kate said. "Since he is staying overnight, we can't ask him about it until morning. It is best that he not have too long to think about it before the ritual takes place, and it's also necessary that he leave immediately after the ritual is over."

"I didn't even tell him Caslar's body is here," Mike added. "I was afraid if he knew, he might not come. I don't think he has sensed anything out of the ordinary around here."

At once word was passed around to all the members of the family that the presence of Caslar's body would not be told to the stranger until the following morning and the wake on this night would be secretly observed.

The ensuing night passed uneventfully at the McCord residence. For hours Angus regaled the visitor with tales of his experiences as a timberman. Although he appeared to be jovial and light-hearted in his recital, he was really crying inside over the loss of his son. A number of times he had to veer away from telling incidents in which Caslar was involved because he did not trust himself to tell of them with full composure.

The stranger appeared to enjoy his stay overnight there and was particularly impressed with the sumptious meals that were served at both supper and breakfast. Although he had heard about the friendly hospitality of the people of southern Appalachia, he had never envisioned it to be as hospitable as he had found it here.

He believed their friendliness toward him was genuine and rightly so for more reasons than he could know about. It was not only their normal way of receiving visitors but also was, in this instance, the careful preparation of a medium to carry away the sins of Caslar. It was their sincere wish that when the time came for the stranger to depart, he would leave without any animosity toward them.

Soon after breakfast, when the stranger indicated he should be on his way again, Kate approached him and said:

"Sir, we would like to ask a favor of you before you go. Although we have tried not to show it, we are in deep distress over the loss of a dear member of our family. His body is now awaiting the performance of a special ritual that our forebears once observed in olden times in Scotland. Maggie here will explain in detail what is to be done and it will take only a few minutes for the performance of the ritual. It is a requirement that you be rewarded for your help and we offer you your choice of a horse or a rifle."

The stranger could hardly believe what he was hearing. Noting the look of sincerity on the faces of the two women, he was both curious and fascinated with their story and wanted to know more about it.

"I am going to be frank in explaining this because the ritual requires it," Maggie began. "Don't be alarmed, for a husky young man like you will have nothing to fear if you agree to help and are honest with us. It is called the ritual of sin-eating. When a person who has committed some serious sins and then dies before receiving pardon for them, this ritual is observed to make it easier for his soul to enter into Heaven. During the ritual procedure, the sins of the deceased will enter the body of the sin-eater. With proper living afterward on the part of the sin-eater, all those sins he acquired will, in due time, be taken away from his body through the absorbing powers of the warm sunshine, the pure gentle breezes and the love of God. The sin-eater may be compared to the Good Samaritan who goes to the aid of a fellow traveler at a time of desperate need. Surely God would find it easy to bless such a person."

The stranger took in every word with due respect for the solemn occasion. In his mind, however, he was skeptical about it all and thought it was just another odd religious practice of these mountain people. Believing there was no harm in it, and realizing he could get a horse to carry him the remaining distance of his journey, he agreed to take part in the ritual.

Maggie then invited the stranger to go with her to a small room at the rear of the house. On entering the darkened and unheated room, the stranger at once became aware of a chilling feeling he had never experienced before. In the middle of the room was a closed coffin and on each side of it was a short stool. Maggie motioned for the stranger to sit on the stool on the left side of the coffin while she seated herself on the one on the right side. Beside her was a small table on which was a tray containing a piece of bread, a cup of water and a spoonful of salt.

Maggie looked at the stranger and, in a low voice, said to him:

"Before the coffin is opened, I want to explain some basic dogmas of this ritual. It is necessary that you, in the position of sin-eater, must not be acquainted with the occupant of this coffin or bear him any grudge. For if you should, the sins you take from him would turn into demons that would torment your soul till the Judgment Day. So, as a formality in our ceremony, do you know, or have you ever known, a person by the name of Caslar McCord?"

"I don't recall the name," the stranger solemnly replied.

"There are to be no mental reservations held about any part of this ritual," Maggie continued. "Do you agree to that?"

"I agree," the stranger responded.

"Also, as soon as the ceremony is over," Maggie added, "you will be given your pay and must leave this community at once, never to return here to live. Will you promise to do that?"

"I promise," the stranger replied in a barely audible whisper.

Thereupon, Maggie gently lifted the lid of the coffin. When the stranger looked upon the body of Caslar, his eyes bulged and his face became deathly pale. Maggie noticed his look of shock and thought it was only a reaction to his not being accustomed to seeing a dead person. The stranger continued to stare in shock and amazement because this was the same person who had taken his money in a crooked poker game in Montgomery only a few days before. A wave of anger suddenly swept over him but he quickly regained control of himself. I must not lose this chance to recover my loss in the poker game, he thought to himself. He now saw this only as a ceremony performed by some superstitious hill people and decided to make the most of it.

After a long pause, Maggie leaned over the coffin, unbuttoned Caslar's coat and shirt and opened them so that his breast was bared. Next, she took the bread and cup of water from the tray and placed them on his bared breast, then poured the spoonful of salt beside the piece of bread.

"Now listen carefully to my instructions and follow them exactly," Maggie calmly said. "Take a pinch of salt and put it in the cup of water. Now take the cup of water and hold it in your right hand. Before you drink any of it, repeat these words after me: 'With this salted water that has rested on your corpse, Caslar McCord, I now drink

30

away all the sins that are upon you. May they pass from your body into mine.' Now pass the cup of water counterclockwise above the head of the corpse three times, then drink a mouthful of water and pour the remainder through the fingers of your left hand.

"Now take the piece of bread, pass it counterclockwise three times around the head of the corpse then repeat the words I now say: 'I break this bread that has lain on your dead body, Caslar McCord, and now while eating a portion of it, I take upon myself your sins.' "

Maggie then instructed the stranger to crumble the remainder of the bread, let it fall to the floor and step on it. Throughout the ceremony the stranger did as he was instructed in an impassive manner, yet within, he had mixed emotions which tried his utmost effort to conceal.

When the ceremony was over, Maggie and the stranger came back to the living room where Kate and Angus were waiting. They both looked at the stranger with a new attitude of cold aloofness as if he were afflicted with a contagious disease.

"Your horse is saddled and waiting for you at the front yard gate," Angus informed the stranger.

The stranger was quick to notice their changed attitude toward him and he sensed an element of fear of him on their part which he intended to use in his own behalf.

"The horse alone is not payment enough for what I have had to do," the stranger replied. "I must have more."

Angus and the two women looked at the stranger in astonishment.

"But when we gave you a choice between a horse and a rifle, you agreed to accept the horse as payment," Angus said with some heat. "We've kept our part of the agreement and we now expect you to keep yours."

With the muscles of his jaws tensed and his eyes flashing with anger, the stranger snapped:

31

"I'll take the horse *and* the rifle *and* two hundred dollars!" As he sat down in a chair, he added: "And I won't be leaving until I get them!"

Angus was dumbfounded. He stood there for several moments and stared in disbelief.

"Give him what he asks for, Angus," Kate spoke up. "He should be on his way."

Reluctantly Angus got the rifle and the money and placed them on a table. Then stepping back a few steps, he said to the stranger: "Take that and go at once! May the Lord have mercy on your soul!"

With a smug look on his face, the stranger picked up the money, counted it and put it in his pocket. He looked at the rifle briefly, then picked it up and, without saying a word, walked out of the house to the waiting horse.

Mike, Cassie and Brian, who had remained in the kitchen during the ritual ceremony, now came into the living room to join Kate, Maggie and their father. There was a common feeling of relief among them all in knowing that the ritual was over and that the stranger had departed. When Cassie looked out the window to watch the stranger leave, she quickly turned and said in a hoarse whisper:

"He's coming back!"

"Well, Thunderation!" Angus cried as he walked toward the door. "Wonder what he wants now?"

The stranger came up to the steps to the front porch and calmly asked for a piece of string with which to tie his rifle to the pommel of his saddle. Brian hurriedly found a leather boot lace and brought it to him. Without a word of thanks, the stranger returned to the front gate, tied the rifle to the pommel of the saddle, then mounted the horse, Caslar's pony, and rode off down the trail toward the mountain pass road.

Late one evening about eight months after the stranger departed from the McCord home, a traveler appeared and asked if he could have lodging for the night. Angus personally stabled and fed the traveler's horse then warmly invited his guest into the house. Later in the evening while sitting with their visitor in the living room before a sprightly-burning fire in the fireplace, the McCords listened with bated breath to the chilling finale of a story they had hoped, as far as they were concerned, had already ended.

The story he heard, the traveler related, was told to him by a man at whose home he stayed overnight on the west side of Powell Mountain. That man stated that one of his sons had come upon a traveler who seemed to be totally confused about directions and appeared to be in dire need of help. He said he and his horse had gone without food and water for two days and nights which was believed to be, at the time, the cause of his disorientation. Since it was late in the afternoon, the son invited the traveler to stay overnight with his family and get a fresh start on his journey on the following day.

While with the family that night, the traveler related a sad tale of personal grief and trouble that had befallen him. Nothing, it seemed, had gone right for him since he came into these mountains. His trouble began, as he told it, when he lost forty dollars, all the money he had with him at the time, in a crooked poker game, which forced him to change his travel plans. Next, he was talked into taking part in a strange ritual in which he allegedly took upon himself the sins of a corpse who, to his great dismay, he discovered during the ritual proceedings to be the same person who had cheated him out of his money in the poker game. While believing himself to be in a position to recoup his loss, he had become greedy and violated his agreement with the deceased's family. Ever since then he had been plagued with one difficulty after another. He was quite sure he had fallen into the clutches of the devil and was totally at a loss as to how to free himself.

The road on which he was traveling had forked on a number of occasions and he had been confused about which fork to follow. After a time he found, to his dismay, he had gone in the wrong direction. When utterly lost, his vision became hazy and he was beset with hallucinations.

He had heard voices near him, he said, but could not definitely locate them. They were, at times, clear and distinct, and sometimes, low and muffled. Yet one word that was clearly heard and repeated a number of times was "Judas," and eventually the traveler, in his confused state of reasoning, believed it came from his horse.

The following morning the traveler still showed signs of weariness from his ordeal of being lost in the forest, yet he insisted on resuming his trip. After receiving some travel instructions he mounted his horse and rode away despite some ominous signs of an impending rainstorm. The family had some misgivings about his leaving under such conditions, but their entreaties for him to remain longer with them were wasted on him.

Before the traveler had gone more than two miles, a torrential thunderstorm enveloped the mountain. Strong winds lashed the trees from side to side, some were partially uprooted and broken limbs were hurtled to the ground. Because of the lashing rain, poor visibility and danger from falling debris, the traveler stopped his horse beside a large oak tree but found no shelter there. When a bolt of lightning struck a tree nearby, the horse became so frightened it dashed away at a gallop with the rider holding precariously to the pommel of the saddle. When they came to a tree that leaned across the roadway, the horse darted underneath it and left the driver hanging there with his head caught in the forks of some branches.

Sometime after the storm had abated, a passerby found the body of the traveler hanging there and hurried to the nearest farmhouse for help. When the passerby, now accompanied by a farmer, returned to the place of the accident, they gingerly took the body down. A full view of its face gave them a shock they would not soon forget. It appeared, they said later, as if it had been struck by the combined wrath of a dozen demons. Both of the victim's eyes protruded from their sockets and the face, now like that of a very old man, was so wrinkled one could have easily laid a finger between the folds of its skin. His appearance was so gruesome that those who saw it speculated he had been scared to death by the devil. It was an immense relief to the people of the community when his body was soon thereafter removed elsewhere for burial.

In a clearing near the place where the traveler so ingloriously died, a man on horseback has been seen on different occasions riding across the open field. He usually emerges from the woods at the east end of the clearing and as he slowly passes across, he gazes all about him as if he is lost. His horse is similar to the one the wayfaring sin-eater had and there is a rifle tied to the pommel of his saddle. When he reaches the western end of the field, he turns in his saddle and looks back for several moments, then enters the woods and disappears from sight.

Some of those who have witnessed the appearance of the man on horseback believe it is the ghost of a Confederate soldier disguised as a civilian to protect his identity; others say it is the ghost of the wayfaring sin-eater. Those who knew the full story of the sin-eater believed he was destined to keep riding on his lonely journey without surcease until he arrived at the Judgment Day.

Restless Spirits on Droop Mountain

Atop Droop Mountain, whose crest is three thousand feet above sea level, is located Droop Mountain State Park. It was established as a lasting memorial for those men, both Union and Confederate, who fought and died in battle there during the Civil War. In the annals of that war, the event that occurred at that place is of minor significance; however, it does rate as probably the most important military activity that the state of West Virginia experienced during that conflict. The location overlooks the lush valley of the Greenbrier River, the Little Levels of Pocahontas and a number of far-off peaks of the high Alleghenies, making it one of the finest scenic views in this area of Appalachia. To most passersby, the place is one of quiet seclusion and serenity, but for some of those who have lived there any extended length of time, it is often disturbed by the restless spirits of those who died there on that long ago November day in 1863.

Reports of sighting of spirits in this area were made long before the battlefield state park was dedicated there on July 4, 1928. In subsequent years, practically all park superintendents there, or members of their families, have either seen or heard the spirits or have had direct reports from others who have witnessed the strange events.

Near dusk one evening while the children of the park superintendent were playing on the front lawn at the park office, they distinctly heard the sound of some horses approaching. Their father, who was in the office at the time, also heard the sound and hurried outside to see what it might be. While he and his children stood there in total wonderment, some invisible horses trotted past them on the road nearby.

On another evening at the same place, it was reported that what was believed to be the faint sound of a bugle was heard to come from the northwestern part of the park. After an interval of a few minutes, the clatter of feet of several horses was heard approaching from the direction whence the bugle sound had come. Louder and more distinct the sound became as the invisible horses approached and trotted past the park office. Soon the spirited clatter of hooves gradually diminished as the phantom cavalry continued on the road southward through the park.

One day while Carole Holbrook, the six-year-old daughter of the park superintendent, Nat Holbrook, was playing among some pine trees at the front of the superintendent's residence, she was surprised to see a man in a knee-length Confederate coat sitting on the ground with his back leaning against a tree and apparently asleep. She ran in the house to tell her mother and when they returned to the spot where the sleeping soldier had been seen, they found him gone.

On another day while Mrs. Holbrook was busy with her housework, she heard footsteps on the back porch. When she went to the back door and looked out, she saw no living thing; however, she heard steps on the walkway going toward the cellar, which was situated near the back porch. The sound of the steps continued up to the cellar door and was followed by the jingling of the cellar door lock. Then there was total silence.

A number of people who have lived in the vicinity of the park have reported hearing screaming noises that have come from various points in the surrounding wooded area. Invariably it is the agonizing sound of a human being in distress. Thorough searches of the areas immediately following such frightening disturbances have failed to locate the origin of the cries.

In 1920, eight years before this memorial park was established, Edgar Walton and a friend were in the area one night and while preparing to build a fire they were amazed when they saw a headless form float past them. At a later time while Walton, two of his daughters and a son-in-law were in the same location cutting firewood, they saw another headless apparition. This one was wearing a gray-colored uniform; it floated along near where they stood and then disappeared behind some bushes. All of them said they distinctly heard it groan as it passed by.

Another family that has witnessed several appearances of the ghostly spirits of Droop Mountain is that of Mr. and Mrs. Floyd Clutter, caretakers of the park for several years. About ten o'clock one night in July 1977, Floyd and his wife and some relatives, on their return to the park residence from church services, went to the kitchen for a snack. While they were eating, they heard footsteps on the front porch, then the sound of the front door opening. Next came the sound of voices of several young people that seemed to be coming into the living room. Floyd was quite sure he had locked the front door when they returned home. Now he was curious to know who these people were and how they got in the house. He arose and hurried to the living room but saw no one there. It was also observed that the front door was still locked.

On another night about a month later that summer while Floyd was visiting a friend, Mrs. Clutter was sitting at home alone watching television. Abruptly the quiet of the night was interrupted by a loud knocking on the outside wall of the house back of the television set. Thinking it might be her husband trying to scare her, she hurried to the window and cautiously peered out into the front lawn area. By the light that came from the front porch, she saw a hat float past the window where she stood and then watched it drift away into the darkness. For several minutes a quiet, eerie silence followed and nowhere could she see any evidence of the cause for the knocking on the wall she had heard.

One day while visiting at the Clutter home, Floyd's mother saw a man standing in the area of the soldier's grave back of the caretaker's house. For several moments he stood there gazing down at the graves in deep meditation. Then suddenly looking up, he slowly stepped over behind the tree and disappeared from view. After waiting several minutes for him to reappear on one side of the tree or the other and failing to do so, Mrs. Clutter went out to see about him. A cursory check of the area failed to locate him and she concluded that it had been an apparition for there was no way a real person could have disappeared so easily.

There seems to be no end to the reports concerning the spirits on Droop Mountain. Among the most recent ones have been the hearing of invisible horse-drawn wagons that nearly ran down some pedestrians on the roadway; some sharp military commands that were preceded and followed by eerie silences; and the sensing of the presence of something evil in one of the bedrooms of the caretaker's residence without anyone being able to see or identify it. Everyone who has been a witness to these phenomena seemed assured that the spirits on the mountain are, indeed, a restless lot and the reason for their restlessness is a question that presently has no answer.

Ghostly Capers in an Old Farmhouse

When Josie Alden died in June 1974 at the old homestead on lower Slaty Fork, that event marked the beginning of numerous tales being told about the place being haunted. Even after all the noises that were made by some bats in the attic and the scraping of limbs of a nearby tree against the metal roof of the house were taken into account, there were other noises and the sighting of fleeting objects that could not be explained.

On the afternoon following Josie's burial, her son, David, with his wife, Eva, and their four-year-old son, Allen, made a visit to the old homeplace. Allen had not been taken to the funeral of his grandmother; in fact, he did not yet know she had died. Since he suffered from a heart condition, his parents felt that special precautions would have to be taken in breaking the sad news to him. Moreover, the close relationship Allen had had with his grandmother had been a sustaining factor in his survival thus far. He adored her and had insisted on being brought to the old homestead to see her.

During the time of Josie's final illness, little Allen had not been taken to see her because his parents did not want him to know of her eccentric behavior. They did not know how to explain to him about her sudden lapses of memory when she did not recognize anyone; or how she struggled with her housekeeper and then, pouting like a small child, would go to the top of the stairs and sit in silence for hours at a time.

40

On this day of their visit to the old homeplace, Allen got out of the car and ran ahead of his parents to the house and went inside. Still doubtful about how to handle the situation, David and Eva stopped on the front porch and wondered what Allen's reaction would be when he would not be able to find his grandmother. Presently, they heard him call out to them from inside the house: "Mama, Daddy, come here quick!"

On entering the living room they saw Allen standing at the foot of the stairs with a worried look on his face.

"Why is Gramma sitting at the top of the stairs?" he inquired. "Why won't she talk to me?"

Incredulous, they both ran to the stairway and looked up but could see no one. Yet at that very moment they heard footsteps crossing the floor of the room overhead. All three then hurried upstairs and looked in all the rooms but could find no evidence that anyone had been there.

As they came back down the stairs, Allen inquired of his parents:

"Where did Gramma go?"

After they calmly explained to him that his grandmother had gone away, he has never sought a fuller explanation. As of this writing, he still believes he was the last person to see her before she left.

Strange noises have continued to be heard in and about the old farmhouse. Although David and Eva had inherited the place and planned to make it their home, a stay there of only one night was enough to convince them that the place was haunted and that no comfort or rest could be found there.

When some friends of David and Eva doubted the existence of ghosts and laughed at the tales that had been told about the old farmhouse, they were invited to spend a few nights there by themselves. The invitation was jovially accepted with the intention of their living in the house for

41

at least a week. Surely, they thought, that should be sufficient time to prove that the house was not haunted.

The first thing the friends did on their arrival at the old farmhouse was to go through all the rooms, both upstairs and downstairs, to see if there was any evidence of some practical jokes awaiting them. When satisfied there were none, they switched off the lights and retired for the night. Soon thereafter they heard the patter of feet running across the bedroom floor upstairs and guessed it to be some rats capering about. This was soon followed by some scraping and rumbling noises that were similar to that made by furniture being moved about. Knowing that such a noise could not be made by rats, they suspected that some friends might have used a ladder to enter the house through an upstairs window and were trying to scare them. They hurriedly put on their robes and went outside to investigate with the idea of removing any ladder they might find there. However, they walked all the way around the house but no ladder was to be seen thereabouts. It was observed, also, that all of the upstairs windows were closed.

Now thoroughly intrigued, they went back inside the house, turned on the lights and went stealthily upstairs. By this time the strange noises had stopped, but a most unusual sight awaited them. They were astonished to see that all the furniture in the upstairs bedroom had been rearranged. After furtively looking into the clothes closets and under the bed without finding anyone, they ran back downstairs, quickly collected their belongings and hurried away to their own home. The latest report was that the old farmhouse was still begging for a tenant.

The Mystery of the
Door Lock

A few years ago when Larry Stephens, a traveling sales-
man, and his wife, Ellen, moved to Parkersburg, they
were pleasantly surprised to be able to locate a house in
which to live so readily after their arrival there. It had
been their experience in the past to have to spend days,
even weeks sometimes, before locating a suitable place to
live. Because of the nature of Larry's profession, frequent
transfers, along with the usual difficulties of moving,
were expected by the two. Ordinarily, they made a careful
evaluation of the neighborhood in which a prospective
house was located, but in this instance, they were so
pleased with the house and its environs they saw no
reason for a check on it.

The house they rented was situated on the outer fringe
of the suburbs. The nearest and only other house on their
street was about a half-block away toward the city. The
wide open spaces, the clean air and the absence of any
disturbing noises seemed to make the neighborhood an
ideal place in which to live. So it was with happy hearts
Larry and Ellen moved into their new home.

When the time came for Larry to prepare for an extended trip away from home, he told Ellen he would feel
better about leaving her there alone if a new lock was installed on the back door of their house. So, he at once
drove into town to a hardware store and bought a lock for
the door.

On his return home he immediately began to install the

lock but soon found that a piece was missing. Since another trip to town for the missing part would delay his leaving on his trip, Ellen suggested that he should go ahead and she would get the missing part and complete the installation of the lock.

Soon after Larry departed, Ellen drove to the hardware store where the lock had been purchased and obtained the missing part. On her return home, she was baffled when she saw that the lock had been completely installed during her absence, including the part that had been missing.

Now somewhat upset by the turn of events, Ellen ran out to her neighbor's house to make some inquiries. She soon learned, to her dismay, that her house was haunted and that as long as the neighbor could remember, no one had ever lived there very long.

Ellen immediately went to live with some friends until Larry returned home and they never went back to the haunted house to live.

Respect for a Specter

When Marcia Levine of Connellsville, Pennsylvania, was a little girl, she was a witness to an experience that still remains vividly in her memory. She has said it was so real in every little detail it could not possibly have been a product of her imagination.

One day Marcia's mother asked a house painter to do some interior painting in their house. Soon after the work was begun, some problems developed which put a severe strain on the relationship between Mrs. Levine and the painter. Marcia's mother, it seems, was a perfectionist and was quite difficult to please while a decision was being attempted on the choice of color of paint to use. For some time the painter tried to be as diplomatic as his nature would permit but after a number of beginnings of painting were halted by her, he became quite upset. Thenceforth he refused to talk directly to her and would communicate only through the little girl, Marcia.

The painter was thoroughly dedicated in his work and wanted his customers to be fully satisfied; otherwise he would have given up on this assignment. Finally, he was able, through Marcia, to get Mrs. Levine to agree to the use of a particular color of paint. For the next day or so, he worked without any interruption or interference on the part of Mrs. Levine. When all the painting had been completed except the wall back of the open stairway, the painter suddenly became ill and had to go home. Before leaving, he asked Marcia to tell her mother he would return and finish the work as soon as he felt better.

When word came a few days later that the painter had

45

died, both Mrs. Levine and Marcia were shocked. It was especially a sad experience for Marcia because she had acquired a sincere respect and liking for the man.

A short time after the painter's death, a specter of him appeared on the stairway in the Levine's living room one day when Marcia was there alone. It was wearing white bib-overalls and a white cap like those the painter had worn and in its hands were a pail of paint and a brush.

"I just had to come back to finish painting this wall," Marcia thought she heard the specter say.

Marcia was surprised to feel no fear of the specter and found it easy to converse with it. Much in the manner she had talked with the painter when he was alive and working there, she now explained to the specter that there was no further commitment on its part; she felt sure her mother would be able to get someone else to do it. Marcia praised the work that had been done and told the specter not to worry about the unfinished work. At the conclusion of her remarks, the apparition quickly disappeared.

The Wages of Indolence

The Claud Kelly farm covered a thousand acres of rolling hills and valleys, woodland and meadows, grain fields and pastures. In addition to the comfortable farmhouse that was situated near the center of the farm, there were other dwelling houses located on it, some of which had served as living quarters for slaves before the Civil War. This Kelly family, in earlier generations, had inherited some slaves while living in eastern Virginia. Since there was a firm family policy of opposition to selling slaves and since they could not free them because a state law forbade the manumission of slaves, they were brought into western Virginia when this family migrated here.

Even after the day of freedom came for them, the elderly Negroes on the Kelly farm, in their bewilderment, insisted on remaining there rather than venturing out into a strange, though free, world. Thenceforth they lived out the remaining years of their lives there as self-employed free renters. As each Negro dwelling became vacant, steps were taken soon thereafter to raze it and thus remove a former mark of slavery from the land.

On the day following the burial of the last of these former slaves, Claud Kelly sent two of his sons, Pete and Lloyd, out to begin the work of tearing down the house that Negro had occupied. Soon after arriving there, the two teenaged boys were interrupted in their work when they heard a voice telling them not to tear the old house down. Looking out toward the road, they saw coming toward them a one-horse-drawn rickety wagon loaded with odds and ends of shabby furniture. Walking alongside and behind were a man and woman and half a score of ill-clad children. The boys recognized them to be the Mont Tabor family from the Pigeon Creek section of the county.

Mont explained that the house in which his family had been living had burned with much of their household goods and they now were in desperate need of shelter. Until a better place could be found, he said, he hoped he could settle his family in the old slave house. Pete, the older of the two Kelly boys, explained that although his father had his mind set on razing the house as soon as it could be done, it was possible, under the circumstances, that he might postpone having that done until a later time. So, after a brief visit to the Kelly residence, Mont returned grinning from ear to ear, and told his family to unload the wagon and carry their belongings into the house.

Thereupon, Pete and Lloyd returned home not the least disappointed at the turn of events. Yet, they were surprised when they heard their father say he had consented to the settling of the Tabors on his property against his better judgment, a remark they would have occasions to recall all too often in the future.

Although the Tabors had moved in on a warm day in March, several days passed during which time they made no effort to seek another place to live nor indicated an interest in putting out any gardens or field crops. At length, Claud went over and suggested to Mont that in view of his not finding another place to move to, the land in the vicinity of the house where he lived was his to use for the growing of foodstuff for his family if he so desired. Then, in the event another house could be located later in the year, he could still harvest his crops and take that with them when they moved. Moreover, Claud offered him a variety of vegetable seeds and the use of a plow if he should be interested. Mont appeared to give some thought to the idea and reluctantly accepted Claud's offer of assistance.

During most of the summer the Tabors remained aloof and seemingly idle much of the time. There were occasions when some of the smaller Tabor children would be seen poaching eggs from the Kelly barn or sneaking out the far end of the corn patch with a few ears of sweet corn. Such minor thefts were overlooked at the time and seemingly soon forgotten.

Summer passed to fall and fall to winter and the Tabors were still there. More than once, members of the Kelly family wondered out loud how they were surviving. It was well-known that the results from the puny efforts they had made toward the raising of foodstuffs for themselves had been meager and far from adequate for the needs of such a large family.

Near daylight one morning Claud's daughter, Charity, went to the smokehouse nearby to get some meat for breakfast. As she reached out to open the smokehouse door, a person carrying a ham came bolting out of the building and knocked her sprawling into the grass. She was so winded and scared, she lay there several moments trying to cry out but could make no sound. After a time, she was able to recover her breath sufficiently to call for help. Soon other members of the family came running out and helped her back to the house. The family was not too surprised when she said she was sure the thief was the oldest of the Tabor boys.

Claud was thoroughly angered by this act of stealing and decided the time had come for him to tell the Tabors to move out. In high dudgeon, he set out to perform a task that was not at all to his liking. On the way there, he came upon one of the smaller Tabor girls who, while wearing her father's boots, had become helplessly mired in a mud puddle in the road out of sight of her house. She was not crying nor making any sound but her big blue eyes glistened with tears. When Claud leaned over and lifted her out of the boots, she threw her arms around his neck

49

and hugged him tightly. Then retrieving the boots from the mud, he carried them and the little girl to her house. So affected was he by this incident, he never mentioned to the Tabors the real reason for his visit that day.

In the days that followed, the Kelly boys tried to keep a closer watch about their homestead. While talking with some other young people in the neighborhood, they learned that certain other families had been missing certain items of foodstuffs from their cellars, smokehouses and granaries. At length, it was decided something would have to be done, if not to get the Tabors to move, at least to try to restrain them in their pilfering activities.

It was suspected that most, if not all, of the stealing was being done by the older children while aided and abetted behind the scene by the parents. So, it was agreed that an effort would be made to restrain them through the power of superstition. Whenever they met the Tabor children, inquiries were made whether they had heard any strange noises about their house. They then proceeded to relate to them how the Negroes, while living there, had spoken of spooks, poltergeists and even devils being heard or seen in and about the place where they lived.

Late one night, two of the Keffer boys who lived on a neighboring farm, stealthily crept up to the Tabor house. After assuring themselves that the family was asleep, they quickly attached one end of a long piece of twine to the outside wall at the back of the house. Then while hiding behind some shrubbery, a few yards back, they pulled the twine taut and prepared to stroke it with a piece of resin. At that moment, there came an eerie moaning sound from the house that soon caused considerable excitement both inside and outside the house. While some of the members of the Tabor family were running out the front door, the Keffer boys were fleeing from the back yard because the noise they heard was not of their making.

Soon thereafter it was learned that the Tabor children were so alarmed over the tales they were told and the noises they had heard, they were afraid to venture out of their house at night. Reported incidents of pilfering became rare and it was believed the plan of intimidation was paying off. Nevertheless, a lookout for suspects continued as a means to detect any resumption of thievery if it should occur.

One night a few weeks later, the Keffer boys saw Mont Tabor, with a rope in his hand, go into their barn. What he might be planning to do with the rope was not known to them, but the possibilities of what he could do made them angry and very excited. While expecting momentarily to see him come out of the barn leading one of their horses, or a cow or calf at the end of his rope, they were totally surprised to see him emerge with a huge bundle of hay on his back. They guessed he must have been getting both wary and desperate to travel at least a mile from his house to get hay for his horse.

As the boys watched Mont trudge slowly up the hill on the way toward his home, they decided to give him a scare that would stay with him awhile. They quietly followed him up the hill, always keeping behind far enough to be out of his sight and hearing. Then just as he neared the top of the hill, one of the boys crept up close behind him and lit a match to his load of hay. As the flames of fire blazed up Mont quickly released his hold on the hay and ran screaming down the other side of the hill. Seemingly unknown to him, the rope which he had used to hold the bundle of hay together, in some way was still attached to him and trailed behind, occasionally thumping his heels in his wild running spree.

Pete and Lloyd, who were in the vicinity of the Tabor house at that time, heard Mont coming toward his house, still screaming and panting heavily. As he ran up

51

the steps to his front door, they heard him exclaim: "Quick, bar the doors! I tell you Hell is not half a mile from here and the Devil himself has dogged my heels every step of the way home!"

At the breakfast table the following morning, Claud said to his boys: "The Tabors moved out sometime during the night, so I want you to tear that old house down today. This time we won't let anyone talk us out of it."

An Indelible Spot
of Blood

No one will ever know exactly what occurred on that cold winter night when a wayfaring stranger froze to death on the front porch of the Eskew house. A great deal of speculation has arisen about the tragic incident, some of which could be closer to the truth of the matter than some people would like to believe. Moreover, subsequent occurrences at the old Eskew place have only added to the bizarre nature of the incident as if to make assurance that those who knew of the tragedy would not be allowed to forget about it.

On that bitter cold night in late January, a wayfaring stranger had come into the community wading through knee-deep snow along the highway. For more than a mile to a junction of a sideroad with the highway, his tracks were traced on the day following the incident, but from that point there was no evidence to indicate from where he had come. His first tracks were plain and separate as if he had lifted his feet high as he stepped into the deep snow. Soon, however, it was noticed that his feet were dragging through the snow as if his legs were becoming stiff from the freezing cold. There were places where it appeared he had fallen down and then had struggled to his feet and forced himself to continue on his journey.

The first habitation of any sort that was to be found along the way he passed that night was the Eskew place. While within sight of that house, he had fallen into the snow several times as he approached and it was surmised that he had been progressively growing number throughout his body. With great effort he had forced himself up the walk to the front porch of the house and there he fell for the last time. With his outstretched right arm he barely reached the door and scratched his numb fingers against it until he lost consciousness.

Inside the house, the Eskew family had retired for the night and the scratching noise on the front door awakened them. It was reported that they thought the scratching noise was being made by a stray cat or a wild animal and they made no effort to see what it might be. Then dismissing the incident as being unimportant, they went back to sleep and thought no more about it until the following morning. Soon after the event occurred a rumor circulated about the community that some members of the family did look out a window and saw the man lying there. On the basis of past experience, they believed he was either drunk or an escapee from a nearby mental asylum. In either case, they thought it might endanger the family to bring such a person inside the house; therefore, no effort was made to help him. The next morning when they found that the man had died at their front door, their remorse for failing to help him at a time of dire need was overwhelming.

Since that incident occurred, a number of strange and unexplained noises have been heard about the place. One disturbing and often repeated noise was a scratching on the front door, but when the door was opened, the scratching stopped and there was no evidence to show what was causing it. Also, some have said they have heard a crunching sound in the front yard, in both winter and summer, which was similar to that made by a person walking through crusty snow.

The strangest, and most obvious, phenomenon was the reappearance of a spot of blood on the front porch where the unfortunate man had cut his head when he fell.

Although the spot had been scrubbed away several times, it always returned the following night. To see the blood spot there was a sad reminder to the family of the tragedy that had occurred there and it bore heavily upon their conscience. After all their efforts had failed to remove it, the porch was torn down and burned and a new one was built in its place. Since then, all has been quiet in and about the old Eskew place.

A Journey Back in Time

When Frank Holliger was twenty-three years old, he left his family farm in the hills of West Virginia and went to Washington to work in the Post Office Department. To get there, first of all, he had to walk some fifty miles from his home to the nearest railway station at Charleston. From there he traveled eastward on the first train he had ever seen. Although his parents were saddened to see him go, they were proud of his success in getting a position in the civil service of the federal government.

In the years that followed, Frank married and lived with his growing family in a suburban section of the city. He was so dedicated to his work he rarely took vacations and returned to the place of his youth only once. That was the occasion when he went to accompany his aged parents back east where they were to live out the remaining years of their lives in his home. Nevertheless, Frank did not forget his heritage. On many occasions he told his family about his experiences while a boy on his parents' farm. Among other things, he spoke of the isolated location, the constant struggle to keep the farm cleared from an encroaching wilderness or as he called it, "fighting back the brush," the ever-present worry about diseases and the numerous home remedies for them, and the customs and superstitions of the people who lived there.

These stories made a deep impression on Frank's eldest son, Rob. Upon his graduation from high school, he decided to visit the place of his father's youth. On his arrival there he found, to his great surprise, that much of what his father had told him was still to be found there. The people lived in an isolated world all to themselves. Most of them had never heard of a high school and there was none of that rank to be found within a radius of fifty miles of that community.

Rob went to his father's old homeplace and found the log house still standing although the roof had partially fallen in. The barn and some other outbuildings were in similar poor condition. He learned that after his grandparents had moved away, the Chet Jones family had lived there for a time before moving to a new log house they had built at the southwestern edge of the farm about a half-mile away.

While visiting the old homeplace, Rob went down to a cave in a ravine nearby where his grandparents had a cellar house. He found the cave in a secluded spot the entrance to which was sheltered by an aged and gnarled beech tree. The cellar house was quite like his father's description of it except it appeared to be a bit smaller than he had imagined it to be. As he walked about inside the cave, he tried to picture again in his mind some of the things his father and grandparents had told him how this cave had been used.

The spring of cool, clear water they had spoken of, and which had been the main source of their water supply, was still there. He found shelves that had been cut into the solid rock sides of the cave where crocks of milk and other foodstuffs had been kept. He recalled that his grandmother had told him the milk would be left there in the crocks until a heavy mold grew on top of it before it would be made into cheese and butter. She had said the mold added a special flavor to the cheese and butter and improved its food value as well. Also kept there had been such other foodstuffs as apple butter, peach butter, sauerkraut and pickled beans all preserved in stoneware jars of varying sizes.

While Rob visited in the homes of the people of the community, many of whom had been close acquaintances of his father during the time of their youth, he was fascinated with the customs, traditions and superstitions that affected their daily lives. He found it to be a common practice by them to keep dried herbs tied in bundles which were hung on wooden pegs in the log walls or from the rafters in their houses and outbuildings. Because of the scarcity of doctors, the people found it necessary to be prepared to take care of their own ailments.

As a way of entertainment as well as a method of educating the youth in the various areas of folklore, including self-medication for numerous ailments, the members of a family sometimes engaged in contests to see who could repeat the greatest number of "sayings." While visiting with one family, Rob found one such contest quite interesting as well as enlightening. This family, which consisted of the parents and seven children, sat in a circle in the living room. The father began the contest by saying: "Hold your breath and bees can't sting you." A child seated immediately to his left, followed with: "When the frogs call more than usual, it is a sign of rain." The next child to the left said: "To keep a dog home, pull three hairs from the top of his tail and put them under the doorstep." The mother said: "When you plant peach seeds, name them after women who have borne many children and the trees will be fruitful." On and on they continued: "Peppers will grow better when planted by a red-headed woman"; "buckeye seeds will keep evil spirits away"; "a piece of wood struck by lightning will cure the toothache"; "singe the hair of a rat and turn it loose and all the other rats will leave";

58

"coughing in the face of a live catfish will cure the whooping cough." The contest continued until the children, one by one, were eliminated and the father soon afterward conceded victory to his wife.

Rob observed that all the members of the family appeared to be quite serious in their participation. In talking about this later with others in the community, he got the impression not everyone believed in all the sayings but preferred to take a passive attitude toward them rather than to question them; it was safer that way.

Some of these people were just as serious, Rob found, in putting their beliefs into practice. Near the house of one family he saw an oak tree stump that had been hollowed out at the top to a depth of five or six inches. He was told that rain water left to stand in the stump overnight was good for the removal of freckles, facial blemishes and warts. The stump water was used most frequently, he learned, by the youth, especially those approaching puberty.

Rob found some of the remedies quite ludicrous. One day while going from one farmhouse across the fields to another one, he saw a small boy standing alone in a cow pasture. On getting closer to him, he saw he was barefoot and was standing with one foot in a fresh pile of cow manure and counting out loud. On the count of one hundred, the boy stepped out. When Rob asked him what he was doing, he said he was curing a stone bruise and that his foot now felt much better. Rob learned it was common for the youth of this area, even to their mid-teen years, to go barefoot during the warmer months of the year. As a result, an ailment often suffered by them was stone bruise. Whether this young fellow ever had a stone bruise Rob had no way of knowing. Moreover, he had no urge to check to see if the remedy had really worked but took the boy's word for it that it had.

Late one evening while Rob was visiting at the home of

a farm family, a young man came running up to the house and said:

"There's gonna be a shivaree over at Gus Brown's place pretty soon. Gus' daughter and her boyfriend just got freshly married and come back there about a half-hour ago. All of you get hold of anything that'll make a noise and c'mon over." He then rushed off to carry the invitation to other farm families in the neighborhood.

This was something Rob's father had never mentioned to him and he was anxious to know more about it. Only a brief explanation was enough to make him believe it was a fascinating custom and he readily agreed to join the others in the mock serenade.

When they arrived near the Brown residence, they saw several people with a variety of noise-making equipment congregated in a ravine below the house. They joined them and waited calmly until all the lights at the Brown home had been extinguished. The leader of the group then asked the restrained celebrants to move closer to the house and while walking around it, to make all the noise they possibly could. Soon a hullabaloo the likes of which Rob had never before heard resounded throughout the valley. The banging of pots and pans, the discordant clapping of horse fiddles, the firing of shotguns into the air and the ringing of a variety of bells combined to create a tumult no person could ignore.

A late addition to the noise-making equipment was a small cannon of Civil War vintage that some half-drunken men managed to roll up nearby and prepare for firing. While some set about chocking the wheels with stones, others began to load the barrel with powder and tamp it with wads of paper. Seemingly unaware that the loading of the cannon was still in progress, a man approached and lit a match to the fuse. Soon after the man who was tamping the barrel was yanked away from his perilous position by a quick-witted bystander, the

60

cannon bellowed with a tremendous roar and carried away the tamping rod with the fiery blast.

At the height of the noise-making, the married couple came to the front door and sheepishly looked out. Although they most likely had expected to be serenaded, it was clearly evident they were very excited and nervous about it. Suddenly two men came forward with a fence rail. The young groom was seized, put astride the rail and carried away while the crowd heartily cheered. After carrying him around the house a few times, they came to a stop in the front yard and let him dismount from his uncomfortable perch. At that moment, the bride and her mother appeared at the front door with a jug of sweet cider and a large pan heaped with gingerbread cookies.

The appearance of the refreshments brought the noise-making to an end and from that point on all was joviality and good humor. The sudden appearance of such an abundance of refreshments was another indication that the shivaree had been expected.

Another common custom of these people that Rob had an opportunity to observe was a wake. When it was learned that a person in the community had died, neighbors and friends immediately took over the various tasks required for the preparation of the body for the wake, the funeral and the burial. Since there were no funeral homes in the community at that time, all of these services were performed at little or no expense to the family of the deceased. While the body was being prepared for burial by some neighbors, others worked on making a casket and in digging a grave. Still others prepared food and brought it to the home of the deceased for the wake.

Rob was invited by some friends to attend the wake with them. When they arrived there, they went into the house and found several people already seated around the open casket in the living room. The flickering light from the homemade candles cast an eerie atmosphere about the room. While some talked in low voices, others prepared to sing some hymns appropriate for the occasion. As the hours of the night passed, the watchers often went to the kitchen where they partook of the abundance of refreshments found there. Throughout the night, the ceremony of the wake was solemn and performed with dignity.

When Rob inquired later about the origin and purpose of the wake, he received a variety of replies. One person said it was a custom that had been brought over from the Old Country and they just kept on doing it without knowing why. Another said he believed it was observed in order to be sure nothing bad happened to the corpse before it was safely buried. Still another responded by saying the main purpose of the wake was to keep a close watch over the body to be certain it was really dead before it was buried.

When there was no apparent heartbeat or evidence of breathing, it was generally assumed the person was dead and while in that condition was bathed and dressed for burial. At that time there were no facilities available for the embalming of bodies. In rare instances, people did revive during a wake and sometimes recovered sufficiently to resume a normal life. At other times, some were not so fortunate. In one instance, in the exhuming of a recently buried body of a woman, it was observed that she had been buried while in a comatose condition from which she later revived sufficiently to be able to comprehend what had been done to her. The realization that she was hopelessly trapped in a grave caused her to become so terrified she had pulled out her hair and clawed and scratched her face until it was a mass of bloody ribbons.

Rob was also told of the time when a boy reported that a spirit came to him in a dream and told him that his big sister, whose funeral had taken place the day before, was still alive. Despite the doubts of his parents, the boy's insistence prevailed; the grave was reopened and the girl was found to be breathing although still in a coma. Within a month after her disinterment, she had fully recovered her health.

One night while Rob was visiting at the home of the Chet Jones family, he was entertained with the relating of some chilling ghost stories, one of which involved the family of Chet's brother, Julian. As background for this story, Chet related that when he was in his early teens, he was overcome by the urge to go west, as so many other young people were doing at that time, so he set out to seek his fortune. After traveling some eighty miles westward, his meager resources ran out and he hired himself out as a farm laborer. Thenceforth for the remainder of his lifetime he resided in that vicinity.

Through habits of thrift and hard work he saved enough money by the time he was twenty years old to buy a portion of the Holliger homeplace where Rob's father had been born. Then marrying the daughter of his former employer, Chet and his new bride lived for a short while in the Holliger farm house. Meanwhile, a new log house was built at the southwestern edge of the farm and Chet moved his family there.

One day Chet was surprised to see his younger brother, Julian, standing at his front door. He had become uncomfortable in a home with nine siblings (three more would arrive later), so decided to follow the example set by his brother, Chet. Under the circumstances, Chet felt obliged to look after the welfare of his brother and shortly was able to help him obtain work on a neighbor's farm.

Unlike Chet, Julian was not overly energetic and saved little from his labor. When he fell madly in love with a young farm girl in the community and they decided to get married, it was Chet who provided a house for them. In the midst of an apple orchard in a cove a few hundred yards below his own house, Chet had another log house built for them to live in until they were able to provide one of their own.

Julian and his new bride, Tacey Jane, spent many happy evenings together while walking among the apple trees that surrounded their home. One particular spot they invariably went to was a rustic bench Julian had made and put under a Ladyfinger apple tree. There they talked of their love for each other and about their plans for the future.

Somehow, their plans did not seem to materialize the way they had hoped. For one, the possession of a house of their own continued to elude them and they were still living in Chet's house when their first child was born. In due time other children came to bless their home while still located in Chet's apple orchard. Yet, in spite of their inability to acquire a farm of their own, they made the best of what they had and their love for each other never waned.

When Tacey Jane died after a short illness, Julian became inconsolable. Despite the entreaties of his children and others for him to rise above his grief, he became so despondent he could neither eat nor sleep. One night he went out and walked among the apple trees where he and Tacey Jane had spent so many happy hours together. The welling up of memories of the past only increased his grief. By the time he arrived at the rustic bench under the Ladyfinger apple tree, he was openly weeping. In fact, his crying was so loud it awakened Chet's family. Chet and his oldest son, Lewis, walked out to where they could look down to Julian's place and in the moonlight saw him sitting alone on the rustic bench. After standing there a short time Chet said to his son: "If Julian doesn't snap out of his grieving pretty soon, he's going plum' batty!''

One night about a week later when Julian still could not sleep, he decided to go out and walk in the orchard again. As he came out the front door, he thought he saw Tacey Jane standing in the yard only a few feet from him. The sight of her there was a total surprise for him and for several moments he was so scared he was speechless. Finally, he got up the courage to ask her: "How did you get back, Tacey Jane?"

"I am not Tacey Jane," the apparition replied. "I am her ghost. I have come to tell you not to mourn her death any more. Her life is over; yours is not. Time will heal your loss and life for you will be good again."

At the conclusion of those remarks, the apparition disappeared. Julian hurried back inside his house and went to bed but did not sleep a wink that night. Early the next morning he went up to Chet's house to tell him about his experience.

"Do you believe in ghosts, Chet?" Julian inquired of his brother.

"I've never seen one," Chet replied, "but that doesn't mean there aren't any. Why do you ask?"

"Well, either I saw Tacey Jane's ghost last night or I'm losing my mind," Julian answered.

Thereupon he explained fully what had happened and added he was not sure what to make of it.

"There Tacey Jane stood, just like she used to look when she was alive and well," Julian said. "I could see her just as plain as if it had been daylight, and she was wearing the same dress I buried her in. Chet, I'm scared sick about this."

"It seems to me you can't argue with the advice it gave you, whatever it was you saw," Chet said with calm assurance. Then he added: "I'd suggest, Julian, that you accept it for what it is and make a new life for yourself."

With the help of his children, along with the members of Chet's family in the days that followed, Julian gradually recovered from his grief. Though he had been thoroughly shaken at the time of the appearance of the ghost, he, in subsequent years, never seemed to tire from telling about it and always made sure to credit it with the saving of his sanity.

Another tale Rob heard gave him the impression that perhaps many so-called ghost stories that were related here in the hills would not be classified as such if a more thorough investigation had been made at the time of their origin. As this story was told, Jake Toler, a young man of the community, had to pass a cemetery while traveling to and from his girlfriend's home. Since the cemetery was located on some land that adjoined his father's farm and only a short distance from their residence, he had never suspected it of harboring ghosts or restless spirits in any form.

One night while Jake was passing the cemetery on his return home, he saw something white some distance back among the tombstones. He stopped and looked at it for several moments but could not make out what it was. Since it made no sound or moved, he surmised it probably was a piece of paper blown there by the wind. Then dismissing it from his mind, he resumed his walking toward home.

A few nights later as the young swain was passing the cemetery, he saw the white object at the same place in the cemetery, but this time it moved and made a blowing sound. With a feeling he had never experienced before, Jake decided not to try to determine what it was but hastened on his way home. The following day while passing the cemetery, he looked again at the place where the white object had been, but nothing white could be seen there. For the first time in his life he felt an aversion toward this cemetery which only increased his suspicion that something unreal was taking place there.

During the days that followed, Jake thought a great deal about the strange thing he had seen and heard but kept his thinking to himself. The next time he went to see his girlfriend, he took a pistol with him. That night as he was passing the cemetery on the way home, he saw the strange white object there and it moved from side to side in a swaying motion. He quickly drew his pistol and fired at it. Suddenly the white object rose up, snorted and appeared to be coming toward him. Now frightened nearly out of his wits, he ran pell-mell all the way home.

The next morning Jake was still debating with himself whether to tell his parents about what he had seen the night before when he went down to the breakfast table. Before he had made a decision about it he heard his father say:

"Somebody shot our white-faced cow in the nose last night. It didn't harm her much, but if the shot had been fired a trifle higher, it could have killed her."

Later, that day, Jake went out to the cemetery to see if the object that had frightened him could have been their white-faced cow. On an elevated spot back of the fence that separated the cow pasture from the cemetery, he found a place where the cow had lain down at night to ruminate and sleep. She had not actually been in the cemetery at all but from the position he had seen her while standing in the road, had only appeared to be in it.

While still at the Jones residence, Rob heard Lewis relate how an attempt was made one night by some prowlers to rob his father of some money. On the day prior to the incident, Chet had sold some calves and lambs to a traveling livestock buyer. Since there were no banks available where the money could be deposited for safekeeping, Chet had no other choice but to hide it at his house. It often occurred at that time that some unscrupulous persons made it their business to keep a close check on those who sold livestock to a traveling buyer. Shortly thereafter they would attempt, usually in the dead of night, to relieve the seller of his newly acquired money. Because of this practice, farm families found it expedient to post guard at their homes for several days and nights following the receipt of such funds.

At the Jones residence, Lewis and his brother, Albert, were given the responsibility of guarding their house during the first night. The teenage boys had two revolvers each with which they were skilled marksmen. Since early youth they had handled guns of various types and on this occasion they felt quite at ease, though alert, while guarding the house. With all the windows covered and the lights out, Lewis sat near the front door while Albert kept watch in the kitchen beside the back door.

For an hour or so, all was quiet about the house except the heavy breathing and occasional snoring of the other members of the family. Then the silence was broken when footsteps were heard tiptoeing across the front porch and, at the same time, the doorknob on the back door began to slowly turn. When Lewis gave an earlier agreed upon signal for action, he burst out the front door and Albert out the back door simultaneously with their guns blazing. The prowlers were so taken by surprise they fled into the darkness. The next morning when an inspection was made about the premises, spots of blood were found on some palings of the yard fence below the house. It was surmised that at least one of the prowlers had been wounded in the nocturnal barrage of gunfire. Although the practice of posting guard at the Jones residence was continued whenever it seemed advisable, subsequent events proved that it really was not necessary.

Before the time came for Rob to return to his home in Washington, he had an opportunity to meet and learn a great deal about Mooney Akers, a unique "character" of the community. Mooney was a scrawny person with wispy thin white hair and beard and looked to be at least seventy years of age when in reality he was under fifty. His eyesight was poor and his voice was cracked and whiny.

Mooney and his wife lived on a small farm but his wife did most of the work there. Before the authorities caught up with him, he preferred to spend his time making home-brewed whiskey, better known in the hills as moonshine and from which the name everyone knew him by was derived. On his conviction he was sent to the state penitentiary for a period of time. While incarcerated there, he did not mind his confinement so much as long as he was being taught how to weave baskets and repair splint-bottomed chairs. One day, however, he was put to work turning a grindstone as partial punishment for an infraction of prison rules and he quickly acquired a different opinion of prison life.

When all the tools the guard had brought along had been sharpened on the grindstone, he informed Mooney to keep turning the grindstone while he went back to the tool shed to get more tools to sharpen. Some time later when the guard returned, he found Mooney sitting on the ground and also saw that the grindstone was missing from its stand.

"Where is the grindstone, Mooney?" the guard inquired in an irritated voice.

"An angel came down from heaven and rolled it away," Mooney replied meekly.

"Well, somebody had better get it back here pretty fast," the guard said. "Any idea who that somebody might be?"

"The angel will of course," Mooney answered. "If you don't believe me, I can prove it to you."

69

From an inside coat pocket he brought forth a small black book, opened it and after peering closely with his beady eyes for several moments, he began to read in a halting manner: "An angel of the Lord descended from heaven and came and rolled back the stone."

"You'd better help that angel get it back here," the guard angrily ordered. "And I mean right now!"

Luckily for Mooney, when he started the stone rolling toward a brush-covered cliff, it had gone only a few feet down the bank and stopped under some bushes. With a display of energy not common to him, he soon had the stone back on its stand and resumed the unpleasant task of turning it.

When the time arrived for Mooney's discharge from prison, he packed his few belongings in a satchel and started home with a deep feeling of relief. Because of the poor transportation facilities at that time, it required three days for Mooney to reach home. While on the way back, he stopped briefly in Parkersburg and went to a hotel dining room for his dinner. The meal was served family style with the food in dishes on a long table with chairs available around it for a dozen or more people. When Mooney went to the table, he sat down in a chair and placed his satchel on a chair beside him.

Mooney ate sumptiously then topped it off with apple pie and sweet cream. While holding a piece of pie in one hand and a cream pitcher in the other, he alternately took a bite of pie and then a lip-smacking draught from the cream pitcher. The mirth this aroused among the other diners brought the proprietress out from the kitchen. She did not see anything to laugh about but demanded that he stop his display of poor manners at once. Then seeing his satchel on the chair beside him, she ordered him to pay for two meals. Still quite unperturbed, Mooney replied:

"If the satchel has to pay for a meal, then it shall have

its dinner." Whereupon, he opened it and filled it with food from the table.

On Mooney's arrival back home, he seemed to have lost all his former zest for the making of moonshine. Since farming did not appeal to him, he decided to do nothing until he thought of something to his liking. At length, he settled on being a pill-peddler. He ordered some patent medicine from a wholesale distributor and walked from house to house trying to sell it.

Since the chief purpose of this medicine was to serve as a purgative, many people saw it as an advancement over the former method of preparing their own dosages from herbs. In a short period of time, Mooney had a clientele of customers throughout the community. Because of his poor eyesight, he had difficulty on occasion in the making of his rounds. It probably was true some of his patrons bought medicine from him only out of sympathy and had no intention of ever using it.

When a farmer in the community gave Mooney a decrepit mule to ride on his medicine route, some saw the gift more as an act of good riddance of an animal that had long since seen its best days rather than an act of sympathy for Mooney. Nevertheless, he accepted the gift with effusive thanks and soon thereafter was assisted in mounting it. With a wide grin on his face, he slowly rode down the country road with hopes of selling more pills.

When Mooney arrived at the next house, he stopped his mule at the yard gate and while holding onto the pommel of his saddle, he slowly slid down the side of the animal until his feet touched the ground. Leaving the mule standing there unhitched, he took his satchel of medicine and went to the house.

After talking with the family for some time, Mooney slowly made his way back to the yard gate. Unaware that his mule had turned about and was facing in the opposite direction from that when he dismounted it, Mooney climbed upon it and sat there for several moments while contemplating his unfamiliar position. With both hands he began to feel about the rump of his steed to try to locate the bridle reins. Then leaning forward as far as he could, he stared in amazement and, in his high-pitched, squeaky voice, piped:

"Heavens-to-Betsy, my dadburn jackass has done lost his head!"

Two young men at the house, on seeing Mooney's plight, suppressed their mirth temporarily and went to his aid. After gently lifting him, they turned him to face in the right direction, placed the bridle reins in his hands, then gave the forlorn looking animal a vigorous swat on the hip to wake it up. When Mooney was out of sight of the house, the glee and laughter that had been suppressed up to that time then found comforting release. One of the numerous remarks made about the incident was that the laughter Mooney's antics brought was probably more efficacious for good health than his pills would be.

When the day arrived for Rob to begin his journey home, he had not realized until then how difficult it would be for him to leave. He had come to love these people and their way of life. Then as he traveled eastward, he had an abundance of time to reminisce about the many experiences of his vacation in the land of his father's people. The more he thought about it the more amazed he became to realize that two cultures so close, in distance, to each other could be so diverse in the manner of living of their respective peoples.

A Pampered Poltergeist

Over a period of several years, numerous reports have been made concerning the presence of a ghost on the campus of Glenville (West Virginia) State College. Its activities have been largely confined to two buildings located on the upper area of the campus and in a cemetery located nearby. Its presence has been of such import that some students, a few members of the faculty and buildings and grounds caretakers have given it serious and discreet consideration.

It is the opinion of most observers of the situation that the presence of the ghost is directly related to a crime that was committed at that location more than a half century ago. In the fall of 1918, a woman by the name of Lou ("Sis") Linn was murdered in her house there by being bludgeoned to death by one or more assailants who were never apprehended. In later years, the Linn property was purchased for the college and on the exact spot where the Linn house had been situated, a dormitory for women was erected and named Verona Mapel Hall. A few years later, another building, now known as Clark Hall, was built in the space between Verona Mapel Hall and the cemetery that adjoins the campus. In those two buildings a variety of activities of undetermined cause have been heard and attributed to the ghost there.

This ghost is said to be a poltergeist, or noise ghost. It seems to delight in making sounds similar to that of chairs being moved about in vacant classrooms; tapping on the plumbing, especially at night; banging on metal wastepaper cans; opening and closing of doors and cemetery gates and a variety of other unexplainable noises. Also, the turning on and off of the lights in the buildings as well as those located over the outside doors and at the front steps has been observed in both daylight and at night.

One student related that while he was working late one night in a basement classroom of Clark Hall, he heard a strange noise upstairs. He decided to investigate and on entering the stairwell that led to the second floor, he reached out to turn on the light switch but before he touched it, the light came on. Thinking that someone upstairs had turned the light on for him, he went up the stairs to the fire door that closed off the second floor hallway. As he opened the fire door, the light went off and left him in near total darkness. The only light to be seen was the red exit light over the door at the far end of the hallway.

For several anxious moments the student stood there pondering his next move. After peering into the darkened hallway for a time he thought he saw an object about halfway out the hall that seemed to sway back and forth. He said it appeared to be about the size and shape of a small black bear. Because of the darkness he could not tell whether it was looking toward him or was facing the exit light at the other end of the hall. Cautiously, he moved backward and began to feel for the light switch without taking his eyes off the swaying object. Before he could find the switch, the light came on and the swaying object and the darkness disappeared simultaneously.

One night while some students were walking past Clark Hall, they saw the draperies at a classroom window open and then close again. The doors and windows of the building were locked and a nightwatchman, who had come from the building only a short time before, said he had seen no one there. At the insistence of the students, he reluctantly went back in for a recheck while the students kept watch at all the building's exits. When the nightwatchman came out, he reaffirmed his earlier statement that there was no one in the building.

A greater interest then developed among the students to keep watch over the area at night. Some took sleeping bags to the cemetery where they maintained overnight vigil while others patrolled the campus until late at night. Shortly after midnight, one student and his girlfriend decided to give up the watch for this night and strolled down the walk beside the cemetery on the way to their respective dormitories. As they were passing the cemetery gate they both were startled to see a dense gray mass slowly rise from a far corner of the cemetery and start moving toward them. At first they were so frightened they hardly knew what to do. After some chilling moments, the young man, who was quite religious, began to pray and to cite verses of the Scripture. When he quoted: "Be gone, Satan! for it is written, 'You shall worship the Lord your God and him only shall you serve,' " the gray mist suddenly vanished.

Shortly after the announcement was made that Verona Mapel Hall was going to be razed, some concerned members of the faculty and students felt that a formal procession of welcome should be performed for the orderly transfer of the ghost from Verona Mapel Hall to Clark Hall. When the time arrived for the ceremony, those who participated in the procession were serious and discreet in their demeanor. Since some of them henceforth would be spending a great deal of their working time in cohabitation with the ghost in Clark Hall, they saw this was no time for levity and gave it a sincere welcome.

Jeanie's Birthmark

The moment I stepped through the doorway of Valjean's Country Store, all who were there stopped what they were doing and stared at me. It was like a picture of activity had suddenly become one of still life. The two men sitting beside the pot-bellied stove, another man bent halfway over and holding in his hands a basket of groceries he had just picked up from the floor, and two women talking to a salesgirl at the counter were all frozen into inaction. They looked at the black loose-leaf book I held in my hand and surmised I was a stranger in their midst who had come there for no good.

When I looked more closely at the attractive, young salesgirl, I was appalled to see tufts of black hair protruding above her high-collared dress. My dismay brought a look of pain to the salesgirl's face and a look of hostility to the faces of all the others who were there. Realizing this was no time to follow through on the purpose of my being there, I excused myself and hurried back to my car. The insurance inspection report I sought required a considerable amount of tact and confidentiality; under the circumstances I decided it would be wiser to postpone the interview until another day.

Before leaving the village, I stopped at a service station to get some gasoline. While the attendant serviced my car, I casually said to him:

"Now, it's none of my business, but I was wondering if you know anything about the young salesgirl who works at Valjean's Country Store."

76

"Like you say, Mister, it's none of your business, so why not keep it that way?" the man calmly replied.

Now intrigued more than ever, I thought about the girl and her problem while I drove back to the city.

A few days later I, with Dale Corbin, a co-worker, returned to Valjean's Country Store for the purpose of making the belated insurance report. We planned for an early arrival there with the hope of getting the information we needed with the least amount of distraction. On our entering the store we saw the young salesgirl and a middle-aged woman standing back of the counter. After introducing myself and my friend, Dale, to them, I briefly explained why we were there. In order not to embarrass the shy salesgirl, we directed our conversation to the older woman who, we learned, was Stella Valjean, the owner of the store, and that the salesgirl was her daughter, Jeanie.

As we went about our inspection of the premises, our questioning was so cordial that any anxiety that may have existed at the time of our arrival there soon passed. My brief appearance there a few days before was never mentioned and I believe Jeanie was relieved that I did not bring it up. At length, our report was completed and the cheerful mood that prevailed at the time of our departure was due, in no small way, to the suppression of our curiosity about the unfortunate girl.

In the days that followed, the curiosity of my co-worker, Dale, did get the better of him and in his spare time, he learned a great deal about Jeanie and her parents. While he related that information to me, it was not difficult to observe that he had an unusual degree of compassion for the luckless girl with the hairy body and the beautiful face. Dale did not tell me everything he learned about the Valjeans, I feel sure, because there were some vicious rumors concerning them that he most likely knew about but refused to repeat. It was not until a few years later that I came to fully understand my friend's protective attitude toward the girl.

At the time Jeanie's parents were married, Dale related, her mother, Stella, was given a pup by her parents as a present. It was a mixture of German Police and Russian Wolfhound and Stella adored it much to the chagrin of her husband, John. From the beginning, the dog was allowed to sleep on the floor of their bedroom on Stella's side of their bed. By the time it was a year old, it had grown to a weight of more than eighty pounds but still was allowed to sleep in their bedroom.

During the first year, the dog became so attached to Stella it chose to become a constant guardian of her person and her welfare. It reached a point where John could not show any affection toward his wife without arousing the jealousy of the dog. After they went to bed at night, John could not even turn over without the dog snapping its teeth at him and growling ominously. Whenever John mentioned to Stella that she should get rid of the dog, it seemed to understand what he said and stared at him with baleful eyes. Despite the fact that the dog was ruining their marriage, Stella would not permit him to be taken away.

On the night that Jeanie was conceived, Stella had locked the dog in the clothes closet of their bedroom. Later in the night, she was rudely awakened by the screams of her husband and a wild commotion on the floor. She quickly sat up in bed and, in the dim glow of the night light, she saw the dog with its huge jaws clamped around John's neck. Stella screamed at the dog and ordered it to let go of him but it appeared not to hear her. With hate flashing in its eyes, it brazenly continued to chomp and break the bones of the choking man. Her empathy for John brought a sharp pain to her own neck and could feel it swelling until she could hardly breathe.

Now completely terrified of the dog, Stella, gasping for

breath, ran out of the room and closed the door behind her. In a state of near hysteria, she ran to a neighbor's house and explained, as well as she could, what had taken place. The man of the house hurriedly dressed, then got his shotgun, ran to the Valjean house and cautiously crept up to a window outside of Stella's bedroom. On looking inside through the partially open window, he saw the dog stop chewing on John and look up at him. With a steady aim, the man fired and blasted the top of the dog's head off. Unfortunately, it was too late to save John.

What Stella had failed to remember when she locked the dog in the clothes closet was the existence of an opening that led from the clothes closet into the towel closet of the adjoining bathroom. It was through that aperture that the dog had found its way out to return to the bedroom for its vengeful attack on John.

In the months that followed, Stella relived the agony of that dreadful night many times. When she became aware that she was pregnant, her worries increased because of the fear that her baby would be a "marked" child as a result of her traumatic experience. The few friends Stella confided in did little to relieve her of her fears because they, too, were fearful for her child and made no effort to conceal it from her.

In due time the baby was born and was named Jeanie. She was a normal baby in all respects except for some tufts of black hair which grew entirely around the base of her neck and on her shoulders. The doctor who made the delivery told Stella the abnormal growth of hair could be the result of a number of probable causes but most likely was due to some hyperactive glandular activity. Moreover, he left the impression that, with proper treatment, it could be corrected. Stella and her friends, however, believed the only cause was her terrifying experience that had marked the beginning of the most depressing nine months of her entire lifetime.

Stella recalled the pain she had experienced about her neck while she watched the gruesome scene of the dog's attack on her husband. She could only believe that the horror of that terrible ordeal had somehow caused the hair to grow on Jeanie's neck. It was to serve as a punishing reminder, she told her friends, of her selfishness in wanting to keep the dog against John's wishes. Also, she believed no attempt should be made to remove the hair because, as one of her friends warned her, it could grow longer and thicker and perhaps spread all over her daughter's body.

After an absence of forty-two months spent in military service, I returned to the place of my former employment to see my friend again. There I learned that Dale's interest in Jeanie had led to his discovery of a cure for her disfigurement. Moreover, their affection for each other had led to their engagement to be married.

On one of Dale's trips through the countryside in the performance of his work, he had heard of a "Yarb Woman" who was said to have magical powers with mixtures of herbs. He found the aged woman living alone in an untidy log cabin in a remote hollow. After explaining to the woman about Jeanie's affliction, she said she was quite sure she could cure her and would have the medicine ready in about a week.

Several days later when Dale returned to the "Yarb Woman's" cabin, she had a mixture of herbs ready for him. She explained that she had taken certain roots, leaves, and fragments of bark of a variety of herbs and shrubs and ground them together to a fine mixture. This she had divided into doses of a tablespoonful of the herbs bound in cheesecloth containers similar to tea bags. Her instructions were that Jeanie should place a bag of the herbs in a pint of hot water and let steep for ten minutes; then remove the bag and drink the herbal tea immediately. The ordeal of drinking the obnoxious concoction was to be performed three times each day at five-hour intervals.

For several days after Dale brought the medicine to Jeanie, she refused to take it. For one reason, she did not have much faith in its efficacy; for another, she wondered, if it did work, how could it remove hair from her neck and shoulders without it also removing the hair from her head. In an effort to lessen Jeanie's doubts about the medicine, Dale returned to the cabin of the "Yarb Woman" for enlightenment. In a most convincing manner she explained that the medicinal properties of the herbal tea would affect only unnatural features or conditions of the body, not natural ones.

After considerable urging on the part of both Dale and Stella, Jeanie reluctantly began to drink the tea as instructed. Within a week's time, it was observed that the unsightly hair on her neck and shoulders had begun to shrivel at its base. Before two weeks had passed, all the unwanted hair had fallen off, leaving the skin white, smooth and soft. Moreover, there were no observable indications of any deleterious side effects from drinking the tea.

Both mother and daughter quickly experienced remarkable changes in their personalities. Stella no longer felt the heavy burden of guilt she had borne for so long but, instead, now felt a warm, inner peace. The change was even more apparent in Jeanie; the once shy, self-conscious girl now became vivacious and outgoing. She explained her indebtedness to Dale for the change by saying he was her Prince Charming who had changed her life from being a freak to one equal to that of the happiness of a beautiful princess.

81

A Victim of Curiosity

Several years ago when Richard Yokel lived in Pittsburgh, he heard of a strange incident that took place near his home and which has continued as a haunting presence with him ever since. It was a tale of how a person whose sudden transformation made him an object of such curiosity he was driven into isolation until only death could release him.

One warm summer night in a suburb of Pittsburgh, two men stood at a bus stop waiting for a bus to take them into the city. Suddenly an electric storm approached and before the men could decide on a place to seek shelter, a bolt of lightning struck the street light post on which the bus stop sign was posted. As a result, an electric power line was broken and one end of the wire fell on one of the men and knocked him down. Without thinking about his own safety, the other man took hold of his friend in an effort to extricate him from the charged wire and in doing so was himself knocked unconscious.

When the latter was revived some time later, he found himself lying on the sidewalk in the midst of a group of curious onlookers. In answer to his inquiry about the condition of his friend, he was told that he had been electrocuted. To compound his shock, he then was told that his own skin pigment had become a peculiar shade of green.

From that time forward, he was commonly known as the "Green Man," and instantly found himself to be an object of great curiosity wherever he went. The staring of the people and the unkind and derisive remarks some of them made about his strange appearance so unnerved him he was forced to go into hiding at his own home. It was only at late hours of the night when the streets were clear of people that he would venture out for some exercise; but this practice sometimes ended in a frightening experience for both himself and any late commuters who saw him. Not only for himself but also for other members of his family who lived with him was the annoyance caused by young children who knew of the "Green Man" and where he lived when they gave the ultimate challenge to their peers, the double- and triple-dare, to go up and ring his doorbell.

At length, he was forced to move to a remote little house out in a sparsely populated rural area far from any other dwellings. There he lived alone while his relatives provided his food and other necessities for his livelihood. Even while living at that isolated spot, there were times when curiosity seekers, who had gone to great lengths to locate him, went out to try to get a glimpse of him. His bitter commentary on the strange fate that befell him was to point out that, of all living things, only human beings were capable of exhibiting such a cruel attitude toward one of their own kind.

They Called It Satan's Baby

Hoy Anderson had been a hard worker as far back as he could remember. At the age of eleven he left home and hired himself out as a farm laborer. Although he had dropped out of school while in the fourth grade, he had a good head for figures and had learned to carefully manage the meager earnings he received for his work. By the time he was twenty-three, he had saved enough to buy a seventeen-acre farm with a fairly decent-looking log house on it near the headwaters of Raccoon Creek. He also acquired a horse, a cow, a couple of pigs and some chickens to stock his farm. As he looked upon his achievements with some pride, he believed he was now ready to go out and get himself a wife.

Hoy did not know any young women in his community who would be interested in sharing a home and a lifetime with him. He recalled having seen some teenage girls while passing a farmhouse a few miles down Raccoon Creek one day and decided to ride down that way. On the pretense of looking for some additional livestock for his farm, he planned to stop at that place and try to get a closer look at the young women he had seen there. So, early one morning in late November as he rode horseback down Raccoon Creek road, he thought about the kind of wife he sought. She would have to be someone willing to do her share of the work on the farm, have good morals and reputation, be frugal in her management of the household and, in due time, bless their marriage with some strong, healthy children.

After traveling about three miles down Raccoon

Creek, Hoy's attention was drawn to a small rundown cottage beside the road from which came a cry for help. He cautiously approached the house and as the cry for help was repeated, he proceeded to open the front door. He found it would open only a few inches because the back of a chair was propped under the inside doorknob. Through the aperture in the doorway, Hoy was able to see an aged woman lying on a couch with a rumpled coverlet spread over her. On her head was a man's old gray felt hat pulled down close to her ears. Beside the couch was a small table on which was an assortment of medicine bottles, cups and spoons. Nearby was a small wood-burning stove.

When Hoy inquired of the woman what he might do for her, she asked him who he was and what he was doing there.

"Ma'am, I'm Hoy Anderson and I'm here because I heard someone in there call for help," Hoy replied. "Did you ask for help?"

"Well, maybe I did," the woman answered. "I hardly know what I'm doing half the time anymore. No one seems to care a double toot about me. Guess I'll just end up dying here."

"If you'll tell me how to get in, I'll be glad to do what I can for you," Hoy said.

The aged woman leaned over and picked up the end of a string that lay on the floor beside her couch. With a vigorous tug on the string, the chair was yanked out from under the doorknob and the door slowly drifted open.

"Come on in if you can get in," the woman invited him. "Since I got sick, I've just given up tryin' to keep house."

Hoy noticed immediately on entering the house that there was no fire in the stove nor did he see any firewood thereabouts. He at once set about getting some wood at the woodyard and soon had a cheery fire burning in the stove. Next, he began to look for some food he could prepare for her. When she mentioned that some potato soup might be agreeable with her, he began at once to prepare some. Throughout the whole time Hoy had been there, he had been besieged with a constant chatter from the woman. To him it seemed that she was more starved for conversation than she was for food.

While Hoy worked about the place, he learned that the woman's name was Retha Bolte and that she lived alone there on her small farm. She told him her son, Chiselchin, who lived in Chesapeake, occasionally came up to see about her. For some unknown reason, however, he had not been up since she became ill. Sometimes in the past when her son was unable to come, his daughter, Meg, would come. Since neither had been there for some time, she seemed to be more worried about them than she was about herself.

"Now that Chiselchin never had a chance after Pap named him that," Retha explained. "On the day he was born, Pap came in and said: "By cracky, that kid has a chin just like a chisel, so that's what I want to name him. Didn't even ask me what I wanted to name him. It's strange what a name can do to a person. Once he got big enough to understand, he didn't want to live around here any more. Wanted to go someplace where no one knew what his name was. So, he went down to Chesapeake. Down there, he is known as C. C. Bolte."

While Retha ate her soup, Hoy went out to the wood-yard and cut more firewood. Some of it he took inside the house and placed near the stove; the remainder he stacked outside near the front door. Hoy performed a number of other chores about the house and became so engrossed in his work he seemed to have forgotten the purpose of his trip out that day. When there was nothing else he could find to do, he told Retha he would have to be going but promised her he would be back the next day to see how she was getting along. She thanked him profusely and added that she felt much better and believed she could manage things for a time.

Now quite exhausted from his work, Hoy decided not to go any farther down Raccoon Creek on this day, but to return home. Perhaps he could resume his trip after he looked in on Retha when he came back the next day, he reasoned. He would wait until then to make up his mind about it.

The next day when Hoy returned to Retha's place, he found her feeling much better. Noting that one of her major continuing needs was more firewood, he went to the woodyard at the back of the house and began to chop more wood for both the kitchen and living room stoves. An hour or so later that morning he saw a young woman ride up toward the front yard gate. Behind her saddle a long white bag, partially filled at each end, was balanced across the horse's back and hung down on each side. Hoy wondered who the woman might be but continued to chop wood. After a considerable length of time, the back door opened and she came out to where he worked.

"I'm Meg Bolte," she said. "And I want to thank you for being so helpful to Gramma. As a small token of our appreciation, I have fixed you some dinner. Please come and eat with us."

While they ate, Meg explained why no one from her family had come up to see about her grandmother. Her father, she said, had contracted rabbit fever when the blood from a diseased rabbit he carried from his belt while out hunting had infected his body through a briar scratch on his leg. He had been taken across the river to a hospital in Huntington where he still remained in serious condition.

Meg explained further that her work as a waitress in a restaurant in Chesapeake would not allow her much time off to be with her grandmother. When Meg asked her if she would consider moving to Chesapeake, at least for the wintertime, she vehemently said she would never leave the old homestead. She had lived her whole life there, she explained, and there was no place in the whole wide world she would rather be than right there.

When Meg offered to pay Hoy for the work he had done for Retha, he refused to take any. At that point he was feeling so sorry for the whole family in their time of trouble he offered to keep a close watch over Retha throughout the coming winter and especially keep her supplied with firewood. Moreover, he told them he would not expect any pay for his work. On hearing Hoy's generous offer of help, both Retha and Meg were almost overcome with emotion.

During the ensuing winter months and into the following spring, Hoy made many visits to Retha's house and saw that she was well cared for. During several of those visits he again met Meg there who came more often after her father died. In time, a bond of affection developed between them and by midsummer they decided to get married.

Following their marriage, Hoy and Meg made their home in his isolated farmhouse near the headwaters of Raccoon Creek. While Hoy worked in the fields, Meg did the housework, took care of the garden, fed the pigs and chickens and milked the cow. As a young child she had loved to do these things while visiting at her grandmother's farm. Doing the same chores day after day, however, soon became boring for her. Also, she began to miss the hustle and bustle of urban living while the solitude of rural isolation sometimes became almost unbearable for her.

As a means to help relieve herself of pent-up emotion and depressive moods, Meg began to seek relief through screaming and swearing. One evening following a long day during which so many things had seemed to go wrong, Meg went out to the milk gap to milk the cow while Hoy worked at the barn nearby. As she sat down on the stool to begin milking, the cow switched her across the face with its tail. Meg's outburst of screams and curses so scared the cow it dropped the cud it was chewing. When Hoy saw what had happened, he ran to the kitchen and got a dishrag to give to the cow to replace the lost cud; otherwise, he believed, the cow might die. After reluctantly taking the dishrag in its mouth, the cow was still so frightened that several minutes passed before she resumed the process of rumination.

Hoy tried to ignore Meg's swearing and hoped she would soon become better adjusted to living on the farm. When their baby, Tessie, was born, Meg seemed to feel much better for several months. She was relieved from doing many of the chores about the farm she formerly did in order to care for the baby. One day when Hoy casually suggested that she resume some of the outside chores, she blasted him with a string of curses he had never heard before. He calmly reprimanded her for speaking in such a manner while in the presence of Tessie.

Later that day Hoy took Meg by the hand and led her to the doorway of their bedroom. He pointed out to her a crude cardboard sign tacked on the door of the clothes closet on which were the words "cuss closet".

"Now when you feel like a cuss is comin' on," he told her, "you go in there and let it out."

Meg burst out laughing.

"You must be kidding!" she said. "You can't really mean it!"

But when she saw the stern look on his face, she realized he was serious about it.

During the days that followed, there were times when

Meg was on the verge of swearing but the thought of the "cuss closet" would temporarily relieve her of her emotional stress. On one occasion, however, when she began to swear, Hoy made her go in the closet and close the door. After a few moments of silence, he heard her say:

"This is silly!" Then she began to laugh hilariously.

When Hoy opened the door, he saw Meg standing there still so overcome with laughter the tears were running down her face.

One day not long after Tessie's fourth birthday, Meg was so overcome with a depressive mood she threatened to leave home and go back to Chesapeake alone to live. Hoy sat up all night with her and tried to talk her out of leaving home but failed to change her mind. Early that morning as Meg walked out the path toward the front gate, Hoy and little Tessie stood on the porch and watched her go. Suddenly, Tessie burst out crying and ran after her mother.

"Mama, Mama, please don't leave me!" she wailed.

Tessie clutched hold of Meg's coat and was dragged along to the yard gate. When Meg tried to extricate herself from the weeping child, Tessie was inadvertently thrust against a gate post and sustained a small cut on her forehead. As a trickle of blood ran down her face and intermingled with her tears, she clutched the fence with her hands and continued to weep and beg her mother not to leave her.

Meg steeled herself not to look back. She felt if she did look back, she would not be able to go through with it. Then placing her hands over her ears to shut out the wailing of her disconsolate child, she ran down the weed-choked road until she passed out of sight.

During the days that followed, Tessie continued to grieve over her mother's absence. Her loss of appetite caused her to lose so much weight Hoy became alarmed at her anemic appearance. He decided he would have to go after Meg and bring her back home. When he told Tessie they were going after her mother, her eyes brightened but her wan smile troubled him. Although he had been terribly hurt over Meg's abandoning them, he was willing to forgive her just to see Tessie happy again.

The next day Hoy saddled the horse, then putting Tessie on the saddle in front of him, they rode down to Chesapeake. On their arrival in town they went directly toward Meg's mother's house. Before arriving there, they saw Meg and a young man walking up the street toward them. When they came alongside, Meg stopped but her companion continued on without speaking.

It was easy to see that Meg was both ashamed and embarrassed; ashamed for having abandoned her family and embarrassed for being caught with a man who was a stranger to her husband. Yet when she saw Tessie looking so frail, a look of sadness came into her eyes. Then taking the weeping girl in her arms, she hugged and kissed her tenderly.

"Tessie has worried herself sick while you've been gone," Hoy said with some bitterness. "She needs you. We have come to ask you to go back home."

For several moments Meg continued to hold Tessie tightly in her arms and made no reply. At length when she looked up at Hoy, her eyes were brimming with tears.

"I'll go back with you," she said. "And I'll try to do better from now on."

On the way back home they stopped at Meg's grandmother's house for a brief visit. Before they left, Retha brought out her Bible and showed them her Last Will and Testament which she had written on a blank page near the front of the Bible.

"Since you are my only grandchild, Meg, I'm leaving everything I have to you when I'm gone," Retha said. "If you and Hoy could see fit to do so, I'd hope you'd

come here to live and even before I go. This farm is big-
ger'n the one you have now and, Meg, you'd be closer to
your Mom then."

Meg looked at Hoy to reply.

"At your age it ain't good for you to live here alone,"
Hoy said. "If you really want us to come down, we'll be
glad to move in."

Meg was highly pleased with Hoy's decision because
she really despised the isolation of the homeplace.
Tessie, too, was happy to hear of their moving in with
her great-grandmother; she had found her to be so much
more affectionate toward her than her mother had ever
been.

After moving to their new home, Meg sometimes became irritable and found it difficult to adjust to Retha's
manner of running her home. Whenever arguments arose
between them, she got the impression Hoy usually took
Retha's side which angered her even more. When Meg
felt she could take no more, she left and went to
Chesapeake to live with her mother.

This time Hoy did not go after her since Tessie was
quite happy to be with Retha and seemed not to miss her
mother at all. Then one day Meg returned home, said she
was sorry for leaving and hoped they would forgive her.
Everyone appeared happy to have her back and they all
made her feel welcome again.

When Meg announced a few weeks later that she was
pregnant, she began to receive special treatment from
everyone in the home. Retha went out of her way many
times to avoid disturbing her and Hoy kept aloof from
any discussions that might inadvertently lead him to
take one side or another.

So passed the days of summer and autumn and Meg
grew in size with her developing child. When the time arrived for the baby to be born, there was such short warn-

ing of its arrival a local midwife had to be called in to assist in the birthing.

While the midwife was in the bedroom with Meg, Retha sat at the bedroom door and waited to assist the midwife whenever called upon. Hoy sat beside the stove with Tessie on his lap. After a long and anxiety-filled period of waiting, they were relieved when they heard a baby cry. Soon afterward the midwife came to the door and asked Retha to come in. Moments later, Retha was heard to cry out: "How could you do such a thing! It's the Devil's offspring! It's Satan's Baby!"

Hoy stood up with Tessie in his arms. When Retha came out he demanded: "What's going on in there?"

"Here, I'll watch Tessie," she replied. "Go in and see for yourself."

Reluctantly Hoy went to the doorway and looked in. He saw Meg lying on the bed silently weeping while the midwife held a baby in her hands. When he approached closer, she pointed out to him that it seemed to be a normal baby girl with the exception of having a three-inch long tail that extended to the rear from the base of its spinal column. While they stood there looking at the unfortunate baby, Meg saw the look of disgust on their faces and momentarily feared for the life of her child. Feeling totally helpless, she closed her eyes and continued her silent weeping.

When Meg was able to be up and around again, Hoy and Retha informed her she would have to take the baby and go to her mother's place to live. To emphasize her displeasure with Meg, Retha brought out her Bible and opening it to the page on which she had written her Last Will, she ripped it out with her gnarled fingers and tore it to bits.

"This place will go to Tessie, now," she said in a quavering voice.

It was a sad time when Meg took her baby and left

home. Hoy, Retha and Tessie stood at the front door and watched them go. The burden of Meg's past mistakes now bore down heavily on her. She dared not look back. The burning tears in her eyes nearly blinded her as she made her way along the crusted roadway. Although she had left home a number of times before, this time was different. After this, she knew, in her heart, she could never go back home again.

A Bewitched Rocking Chair

When Dawson District High School admitted its first students in the fall of 1916, most people thereabouts regarded it as a momentous event in their lives. There were a few in the community, however, who saw no need for any formal schooling above the eighth grade. Any additional education, they believed, could lead one into the clutches of the devil. They averred, moreover, that it would cause the youth to become discontented and rebellious and to leave the community to seek their fortunes elsewhere.

The great majority of the people in Dawson District, despite the dire warnings from the prophets of doom, were gladdened with the coming of the high school. They saw it as an intellectual stimulant for people of all ages in the community as well as a beacon of light that would show the youth the way to a higher level of achievement in their lives. Also, some believed, it would help to bring to an end many superstitious customs, as well as the activities of quack doctors, pill-peddlers, "yarb women," and other questionable practices then extant in the area.

One ardent supporter of the high school was Mark Lively. Although he was in his early fifties, he found it intellectually stimulating to discuss a variety of subjects with the students. Because there had been no secondary school previously available to them locally, many of these students were in their late teens or early twenties at the time of enrolling in this high school. So, to them it seemed like being born again into a world of new horizons and they found it fascinating to listen to

Mark's stimulating discussions. The fact that he was the only person in the community, except for the high school faculty and a couple of medical doctors, to have a college degree, was enough to cause the students to look up to him with respect and some awe.

After getting his degree, Mark had found it necessary to return to the family farm to help his ailing father in its supervision. Although it was initially supposed to be only a temporary arrangement, he never found the opportunity to get away again. Over the years, he so busied himself as a stockman and farmer, he found little time or opportunity to put much of his college education into practice. With the dawn of a new educational era in the community, he looked forward with great expectations to his going to the village where the high school was situated and talk to some of the students after the close of school in the evenings.

On numerous occasions, Mark could be seen sitting on a bench on the front porch of one of the village stores in animated conversation with a group of students. His well-worn bib-overalls, blue chambray shirt and battered, sweat-stained grey felt hat belied his educational background. As he talked, he would bring forth from a pocket a briar pipe with the front part of the bowl burned away, slowly fill it with Prince Albert tobacco and, before the discussion session ended, find time to light it a time or two. Sometimes he became so enthralled in his subject, he would light three or four matches and let them burn to his fingertips before releasing them.

One subject that often came up in their discussions was science versus superstition. Mark had majored in science while in college as a preliminary step toward getting a medical degree that never materialized. On learning of this, some of the high school students went to great lengths to introduce into their discussions items of superstitious folklore which he might find difficult to disprove.

In their discussions, Mark readily disposed of such subjects as the claimed removal of warts by magic; bad luck as associated with black cats, broken mirrors, five-leaf clovers, Friday the Thirteenth and others; the planting of seeds and butchering of livestock according to the signs of the Zodiac or stages of the moon; and the preparation and use of herbs in the treatment of ailments of both people and animals. In his criticism of the activities of so-called "yarb women," he conceded that medicinal properties were found in many herbs they prepared or recommended for use in certain illnesses, but their lack of knowledge of the proper dosage and frequency of use of the herbs could lead to detrimental, or even fatal, consequences for the patient. Mark's use of scientific terms and forcefulness in speaking made his remarks all the more convincing to his audience.

One evening when one of the students brought up the subject of Granny Walker's bewitched rocking chair, they believed they finally had Mark stumped for an answer. Without batting an eye, he said:

"Now that is something I have given a great deal of thought to and I believe I have a logical answer for it. That rocking chair of Granny Walker's really does rock but it is not bewitched; there is a reason for its self-propelled rocking motion when no one is sitting in it."

Mark then explained in great detail what he believed was the true nature of the mysterious rocking chair. He had known Granny Walker for several years before she died, he began. She had been an unusually energetic person right up to the day she died at the age of ninety-one. Even when she sat down in her rocking chair to rest, she kept the chair in motion continuously. She lived alone and no one else ever sat in her chair, not even when visitors came. They knew it was her special chair and

97

they would not dare to deprive her of its comforting motion.

Energy in the human body, Mark continued, is the accumulation of stored electrical impulses. In Granny Walker's case, she was overly endowed with stimuli conveyed by the nervous system and muscle fibers into everything she touched. Even though her rocking chair appeared to the naked eye to be solid wood, it was really porous throughout.

"You all know how porous a sponge is," Mark said. "Well, wood is just like a sponge, only more condensed in its makeup. A piece of wood consists of trillions of atoms held together by some yet unknown force. While Granny Walker sat in her rocking chair, electrical charges of her super energy seeped, or were thrust, into the porous areas around the atoms and in time, energized the chair. Now, whenever that energy through a constancy of motion reaches a disbalance in its positive and negative charged positions, it starts the chair to rocking. When the positive and negative positions become equal in power, the rocking ceases."

Some of the more naive students looked upon this conversation as the highlight of their many discussions with this remarkable man and something they would think about for a long time.

Images: The Jesus Tree

Many of the people of southern Appalachia take imagery quite seriously. Whether an image is experienced in a dream or seen while awake, it is something that requires sober reflection and evaluation. While an image that has been seen may be regarded by some people as a token of approaching fortune, others might interpret it to represent an impending disaster. The history of the region is replete with examples of imagery that have been of such significance on some occasions as to evoke protests, threatened strikes or work stoppages, religious ceremonies and silent wonder.

At the time of the building of the Chesapeake and Ohio Railroad through the New River Gorge, the blasting of rocks from the mountainside in order to obtain a roadbed for the tracks sometimes left images of people on the exposed rock surface. To the more superstitious persons of the area and particularly those who were opposed to the building of a railroad through their community, an image thus formed presaged the coming of something evil into their midst. Sometimes when they saw an image of a person's face that reminded them of someone they knew, they believed that person would soon thereafter be stricken with some misfortune. As a result, some became so overwrought they interrupted the building of the railroad by throwing crossties, tools and other supplies of the railroad company into the New River.

During the road-building era of the early 1920s, Frank Moran was the supervisor of a project to furnish stone for the base of a new road then being built in a section of

99

the Elk River Valley. Even though stern in his appearance and often demanding in his supervision, he was favorably regarded by most of the men who worked for him. There was one laborer, however, who felt he was too often singled out to do more of the most onerous tasks than any other workers were required to do.

One day this man with the persecution complex, pointed out to the other workers the presence of a silhouette of the face of a man against the rock wall of the quarry where they were working. To their surprise they saw a remarkable resemblance to that of Moran, their supervisor. The disgruntled worker told them the image portended the imminent death of Moran. Some of the workers became so disturbed about it, they went to their supervisor and asked him to have the silhouette blasted away. When he told them their imaginations were running wild and should be restrained, they replied that a work stoppage would occur if he did not comply with their wish.

When Moran saw that his men were serious in their request, he gave the order for the image to be removed. After careful preparation, the time came for the blast to occur. As Moran stood some distance away in his usual supervisory manner of leaning forward with his hands propped on his knees and closely observing the activities of the workers, the blast came with a resounding boom. Rocks were hurled in all directions with one of lethal size whizzing directly above Moran. If he had been standing upright, it would have struck him in the head. Soon after this, the disgruntled worker failed to come back to work at the quarry mainly because the other workers advised him to look for work elsewhere.

There is the story of two rural families in an isolated section who had been fussing and feuding for years over the questionable location of a portion of a boundary line that divided their farms. Even though they had not reached the shooting stage, there had been threats of a dire nature made on some heated occasions.

Late one afternoon while some members of both families were engaged in their usual bickering, they chanced to look up and saw a huge silvery cross against the blue sky above them. Although they knew the cross had been formed by the vapor trails of two crisscrossing jet planes, it remained there so brilliant and without any disturbance by air currents for so long they believed it had been created as a special omen for them. Although these two families had not been particularly interested in the practice of a formal religion, they met in a group, knelt on the ground and prayed together. The dispute over the boundary line was soon thereafter peacefully resolved.

In 1972 Ms. Betty Maynard of Logan reported that she saw an image of Jesus on a cross at a church there. Soon thereafter occurred the Buffalo Creek flood which killed 125 people and destroyed millions of dollars worth of property. She firmly believed the sighting of the image of Jesus had been a warning of the impending break in the dam at the head of Buffalo Creek which caused the flooding disaster.

The coal-mining town of Holden, in Logan County, West Virginia, has recently received national attention for being the location of the "Jesus Tree." In late summer of 1982, two brothers, Robert and Matthew Sheppard of Holden discovered the unique image on the tree which stands in an abandoned schoolyard in the town. The tree is some thirty feet tall and is covered with a twisted maze of a kudzu vine which may eventually kill the tree. The image is not too clearly defined in daylight, but, at night, with the street lights shining in the background, it appears to be a striking likeness of Jesus in profile, as seen in paintings of Him praying in the Garden of Gethsemane. The profile is finely detailed

101

even to the delicate cut of its hair and beard. The head is tilted slightly upward with a steadfast gaze toward heaven.

Since the discovery was first reported, hundreds of people have been congregating at the site each day to view the image when darkness comes. Some have come from other states, traveling long distances to view the phenomenon. The first formal church services were held near the tree by a bus load of members from the Verdunville Church of God. Since then many other churches have been busing whole congregations to the Jesus Tree for worship services.

While some people can see only a vine-covered tree and scoff at the idea of an image of anything being seen there, most of those who view it are convinced it is an image of Jesus. Some see the environs of the image tree as a holy shrine where, through prayer, they can find healing power for their afflictions. Cures from crippling arthritis and black lung have been attributed to the image. A number of religious leaders, after viewing the image, have regarded it with awe and believe God's hand is back of its formation for a special reason. Some observers have suggested it could be a sign of the Second Coming of Jesus Christ.

So far, this tree with the unique image has been seen by thousands of curious people. Night after night they come, the old, the young, the sick and the crippled, to stand in silence and awe for hours, and some all night long, in the presence of the Jesus Tree. Whether its powers are imaginary or real, there is no doubt it has deeply affected the lives of many people.

Big Red Returns to Service

The Westerville (Ohio) Fire Department, in 1961, found the protection of the city's rapidly expanding population increasingly difficult to maintain on an extremely limited budget. Some of its members at once set out to find ways to alleviate the problem. As a result, the department bought the chassis of a 1959 used truck, equipped it with a 2,200-gallon water tank and some other fire-fighting equipment and called it a fire engine. Most of the members of the volunteer fire department were quite proud of it and, in time, it became affectionately known as Big Red. In a reference to it in the *History of the Westerville Fire Department* it succinctly states: "It looks very professional."

The continued rapid growth of Westerville brought about a change in fire protection there from a volunteer fire department with unpaid firemen to a full-time paid membership. In order for one to qualify for membership on the new force, a test had to be passed. One member from the old volunteer fire department, who was unable to pass the test, became disgruntled and swore he would haunt Big Red after he died.

After serving Westerville for eighteen years, Big Red was sold to a truck dealer. Some of the fire-fighters were not unhappy to see the truck go because of its age and also its split transmission which made it difficult to drive. There were others, however, who had a great deal of respect for Big Red. One former fire chief tried to talk the city officials out of selling it but all his objections proved fruitless. On the day that Big Red was moved out of the firehouse for the last time, there were quite a few people in Westerville who had mixed feelings on seeing it go.

In 1979 the truck dealer who had bought Big Red from the Westerville Fire Department, sold it to the Panther (West Virginia) Volunteer Fire Department. Panther is a small town in the western part of McDowell County and its fire department provides fire protection for some two thousand people in the town and surrounding communities. After two years of service there, Big Red became more of a liability than an asset. Its brakes and some other mechanical parts were so badly worn they could not be replaced with any assurance of safety. Edward Prince, the fire chief, described the truck as a "deathtrap." Soon afterward, it was taken out of service. After parking it back of the firehouse, some of the members stripped it of all its parts that were still serviceable.

Soon after Big Red was retired, several people in the western part of McDowell County reported having seen the truck roaming the highways, mostly at night. Some have jumped in their trucks or cars and attempted to follow it, but after it topped a hill or went around a turn, it disappeared and returned in its own good time. Before Prince became fire chief, he had heard reports about the ghost of Big Red but never believed them. Then in the fall of 1981, he, his wife and his mother saw the truck near their home. He at once got in his truck and drove to the firehouse, which was less than a mile away, to see if Big Red was still there. As expected, the dismantled truck was still parked behind the firehouse. With so many essential parts missing, it would have been impossible for anyone to take the truck out for a drive. For some strange reason, a fire broke out about four o'clock the next morning in a house only a short distance up the road from Prince's home and near the place where Big Red had been seen.

It was observed that soon after the ghost of Big Red has been seen, a fire breaks out in the immediate vicinity of its sighting. It has proved to be so accurate that whenever fire department members hear that the phantom truck has been seen, they rush to put on their boots and await the fire alarm that they know will soon follow. Fire Chief Prince stated that Big Red is always accurate not only about a fire that is going to happen but also its location.

In order to learn more about Big Red's history, the Westerville Fire Department was contacted. From that source it was learned that the former fire chief there who had opposed the sale of the truck had died about the time that Big Red started its ghostly wandering over the country roads of western McDowell County. Despite its uncanny maneuvers, Big Red is more respected than feared by the Panther firefighters. Fire Chief Prince has categorically declared the department will never get rid of what remains of their magical truck as long as he is chief. Its service as an early warning system has proved to be invaluable to them and it is irreplaceable.

Powhatan's Headless Ghost

The coal mining families who lived in the environs of Powhatan Mountain were reluctant to talk about the headless ghost that was reported to have been seen in a mine tunnel there. Reports on the sighting of ghosts or revelation of any portentous omens that might have a bearing on their future livelihood, were generally ignored. As a protection against the constant danger associated with mining, these people were well-trained to meet the unexpected through a firm belief in fatalism. They believed that what would be, would be and no one would die a day, or even an hour, before his time. Even after the man who was said to have been the first to see the ghost was put in a straitjacket and taken away screaming to a hospital for the insane in Huntington, there still was little said about it. Those who did speak of it openly surmised it was difficult to determine whether the man had said he had seen a ghost because he was insane or because the sight of it had driven him mad. They preferred to think the former allegation was true.

As the story goes, this ghost made its first known appearance on an underground train that transported miners through Powhatan Mountain. On that occasion, while the hoot-owl shift was returning home from work, the ghost entered the train and sat down beside a miner who was riding in a compartment alone. Visibility was poor between the small electric lights that were sparsely strung overhead through the tunnel and the miner was not immediately aware of the exact nature of his companion. The acrid odor of carbide gas brought to his attention that the ghost carried an unlit carbide lamp which was unusual because the miners were then using battery-powered lamps at that mine operation.

When the miner turned on his headlamp, he saw that the ghost was headless. As he gazed at it with growing fright and horror, he noticed that bubbles began to emerge from an opening at the top of the ghost's neck and when they burst, spoken words came out. No one was ever able to learn what the ghost had said because the miner was so hysterical when he came out of the tunnel he was unable to explain the full details of his experience. Although other miners said they had smelled the odor of carbide gas in the tunnel on that occasion, they had seen no ghost or any visible evidence that one had been on the tunnel train.

Later that year, some children of Powhatan were given permission to ride with the miners on a morning run of the tunnel train through the mountain to the other side to gather mushrooms. It was their plan to have their baskets filled with mushrooms in time to return on the afternoon run of the train. Because of the depressed economic conditions of the time, these children were encouraged by their parents to engage in a number of activities that would supplement the families' food supply or income. Since the mushrooms they gathered were sometimes wormy, the precaution was usually taken to string them on wires and hang them over a hot stove in order to remove any worms that might be in them. The probability that a few worms had once inhabited some of their mushrooms did not seem to diminish their appetite for them.

As the train entered the tunnel on that particular morning, some of the children sat with the miners while some occupied a compartment by themselves. They had learned from experience to be quiet, cautious and alert while riding on this train. Even though the chances of an accident occurring were minimal, it was always prudent to be careful at all times. So, on this occasion, practically the only sound that could be heard was the gentle rumble of the wheels of the small coal cars on the metal tracks. After traveling for some time, there was some uneasiness among the children who occupied the separate compartment when they smelled the odor of carbide gas. Then, to their surprise, the headless ghost appeared and silently glided past them.

While the children were discussing, in whispers, what they had seen, the ghost reappeared, tarried a few chilling moments beside their moving car while making some gurgling noises, then disappeared into the darkness of the tunnel. By this time some of the children were so unnerved and frightened they began to cry. The miners in adjoining cars became alarmed on hearing the weeping children but were unable to learn the cause of their distress. It was not until the train emerged from the tunnel and stopped for the debarkation of the children that the other passengers learned of the appearance of the ghost. After discussing the incident briefly, the miners resumed their train ride into another tunnel to the place of their work.

The children spent so much time talking about their experience they seemed to have forgotten the purpose of their trip. Their major worry now was getting back home safely. When one suggested that they could walk back by going over the mountain, that idea was considered no further when another reminded them that that way was a jungle infested with copperheads and rattlesnakes.

When one of the children explained that his grandmother had told him it was a custom in the Old Country to mark a grave for a restless ghost, the others thought it was a good idea for them to try. In short order, they found two discarded mine props and tied them together in the form of a cross with a strip of hickory bark. On the horizontal prop, a boy took his knife and crudely carved the words: Headless Miner R.I.P. The marker was then placed upright near the tunnel exit and around its base were piled some stones to hold it in place. Then feeling somewhat relieved, the children set about in earnest to gather mushrooms.

Later in the day, when the time for the return of the train drew near, the children returned to the tunnel exit. As they approached the site of the grave marker they were astounded to see, at the foot of the cross, a battered, time-worn carbide lamp. Where it came from or how it got there, they would never know.

When the children boarded the train for the return home, they made sure they did not congregate in one compartment but sat beside the miners. Nevertheless, the precaution proved to be needless for the return trip was uneventful. Moreover, as far as known, the headless ghost was never seen there again.

Sid's Haunted Hotel

During the decade of the 1890s, the population of Charleston almost doubled, increasing from around six thousand in 1890 to over eleven thousand by 1900. This influx of people brought many new businesses and additional services to the city, some of which were provided by ambitious entrepreneurs who were among the newcomers. One such businessman was Sid Blackston, who owned and operated a small hotel. Soon afterward, his brother, Horace Blackston, came to town and opened a funeral parlor a short distance from Sid's Hotel. From the beginning, both businesses were favorably regarded and many people sought their services.

After several months had passed, rumors began to circulate that something of a suspicious nature seemed to be taking place at Sid's Hotel. It was observed that some people who entered there for overnight lodging were never seen to come out. Those most often rumored to be missing were pack peddlers, particularly those who had disposed of their wares and had stopped there on their return trip to the east coast. Rumors about the situation became so rife the Ashley Detective Agency was asked to investigate.

Two plainclothes agents of Ashley's came into the city soon thereafter to see if there was any truth to the rumors that had been circulated. Because their initial investigation was circumspect and aloof, they could not find any evidence to prove the rumors to be true. It was decided that a more direct, though dangerous, way to find out would be to send one of their agents, Joe Dooley,

110

disguised as a pack peddler, to stay overnight at Sid's Hotel. Meanwhile, Bill Watkins, the other agent, in plainclothes, would also get lodging there at the same time just to be available in case the decoy agent would need help.

When the day came for the inside investigation of Sid's Hotel, Watkins went in first and registered for a room. After making a careful investigation of his room, he returned to the lobby to read a newspaper and await the arrival of his associate, Dooley. About a half-hour later, Dooley arrived with a fairly large pack of goods and asked for a room for the night. With a friendly smile, Sid asked him to sign the register, then gave him a key to his room. Dooley repeated the room number aloud so that Watkins, who was seated nearby, would know. Then picking up his pack, he went out the hallway toward his room.

On entering the room assigned to him, Dooley looked it over carefully and did not find anything that appeared to be other than normal. However, he sat in a chair all night long, fully dressed, and napped occasionally. Every little noise awakened him and the more disturbing ones brought him to a standing position. The worst scare he got was the sudden outbreak of a squalling cat fight in the alley back of the hotel. When morning came, he rumpled up the bedclothes on his bed to make it appear he had slept there, then took his pack and departed without any untoward incident.

Later in the day, Dooley met with Watkins in another part of the city to discuss the situation and develop their plans further. It was agreed they would wait about three weeks before returning to Sid's Hotel for another attempt to discover the mystery of the missing peddlers. This elapse in time would make it appear that Dooley had sold his wares and was on his way back east to get more goods. It was also decided that Watkins would shave off his beard and mustache so he would not be recognized by Sid.

The second time Dooley registered at Sid's Hotel, he carried a small, but well-packed, valise. This time he was assigned to a different room. As he had done the first time, he conveyed the room number to his associate, who was seated in the lobby, by repeating the number aloud. Then picking up his valise, he went to his room.

On his entering the room, Dooley at once sensed there was something disquieting about it but was not able to determine what it was. He gingerly moved about the room and looked closely at the ceiling, the walls and the floor. On his lifting a corner of the rug, he saw that the bed was bolted to the floor. Further investigation revealed that the bed appeared to be situated over a trapdoor in the floor. After reviewing the situation for several moments, he picked up a heavy chair and tossed it onto the bed. With shocking suddenness, the bed plunged through the floor sideways and the chair was heard to splash into a pool of water in the basement below. He saw that the bed and mattress had remained attached to the hinged trap door while the bed coverlets and pillows had fallen into the abyss below with the chair. Although shaken considerably from the dreadful experience, he quickly regained his composure and returned to the lobby to report to Watkins what had taken place. When they saw that Sid was absent from his usual position at the office desk, they quickly walked out of the hotel together.

The Ashley agents notified the local police who immediately went to the hotel to question Sid about the trap door. After a thorough search, they were unable to find him anywhere about the place. One policeman recalled that Sid's brother, Horace, operated a funeral parlor nearby, so they went there only to find that Horace was missing, too.

What happened to the two Blackston brothers has remained a mystery. It seemed as though the earth had opened up and swallowed them. Some people, thinking along that line, suggested they might have jumped into an abandoned water well in the vicinity that night and drowned or suffocated.

In the investigation that followed, it was suspected that the bodies that were captured in the water tank in the basement of Sid's Hotel were secretly transferred to Horace's funeral parlor, then taken by boat down the Kanawha River to some medical schools in Cincinnati and Louisville as unclaimed bodies. After the investigation was concluded both the hotel and funeral parlor were boarded up and never opened for business again.

Soon thereafter, some people who lived in the neighborhood began to report they had heard strange noises coming from the hotel. The creaking of hinges, the crashing of furniture and the splashing of water were among the noises reportedly heard. But the most disturbing noise of all was the cry of a human voice pleading: "Help me out of here!"

After a time the neighbors could stand it no longer. They went to the city authorities and requested that the hotel be torn down. Within a short time, both the hotel and the funeral parlor were razed and thereafter no more weird noises were heard there.

The Stranding of
Turley's Ghost

In the summer of 1858, Presley Turley, who lived on
Coal River a few miles above Saint Albans, was accused
of the crime of murdering his wife. He was arrested and
transported to the county jail in Charleston where he
would await the convening of the next session of the
Kanawha County Circuit Court. The judge of the judicial
district of that part of the state of Virginia at the time
was the eminent jurist, George W. Summers. Prior to his
assuming the position of judge, he had represented his
section of the state in the United States Congress and,
on one occasion, had sought the office of governor of
Virginia, but without success in that attempt. Judge
Summers was considered to be a highly ethical and fair-
minded person in the performance of his duties as judge.
Nevertheless, there were times when he wished that the
onerous duties of his office could somehow be lightened.
One such time was while he waited for the Turley case to
be heard.

From all the gossip that spread throughout the
Kanawha Valley about Pres Turley's alleged violent action against his wife, Judge Summers knew it would be
practically impossible to find any prospective jurors for
this trial who had not heard of the case and who, also,
most likely, believed Turley was guilty. The law of
Virginia at that time stated that a jury's returning of a
verdict of murder without a recommendation of mercy
made it mandatory on the judge to sentence the accused
to death by hanging.

114

The great concern of Judge Summers over the upcoming case brought him no end of worry. His constant thinking about it affected his eating and sleeping habits and his dreams at night became, at times, wild and terrifying. It was reported that one night he dreamed that Turley came to him and said that if he was hanged, his ghost would come back and haunt the judge as long as he lived. On some nights of fitful sleeping, the judge had nightmares during which he found himself being attacked and choked by Turley's ghost and from which he would awaken covered with sweat and trembling uncontrollably.

After the jury had been seated and the trial had begun, about all Judge Summers could do was to sit and watch the development of the case inexorably come to pass as he had earlier anticipated. Despite his long years of experience in the field of jurisprudence, he now found it severely taxing, at times, to maintain his judicial aplomb. At length, the prosecuting attorney and the counsel for the defense ended their presentations and the jury was sent into seclusion to determine a verdict.

After what seemed to them to be a reasonable length of time for a fair appraisal of all the facts that had been presented during the trial, the jury returned to the court room. Judge Summers looked at the jury foreman and solemnly asked: "Has the jury reached a decision?"

"We have, your honor," the foreman replied. "Guilty, as charged, without recommendation of life imprisonment."

Judge Summers felt numb throughout his body. He watched coldly as the bailiff asked Turley to stand to receive the judge's sentence. Then as though listening to the ominous words of an unknown person he heard himself say: "Presley Turley, I now sentence you to be hanged by the neck until you are dead."

Soon after the trial ended, Judge Summers met with

the high sheriff of Kanawha County to make a decision on the location for the hanging of Pres Turley. At that time the population of Charleston consisted of only a few hundred people who were mainly congregated in the area where portions of the presently named streets of Summers, Capitol, Dickinson, Brooks, Morris, Court, Virginia and the Boulevard (then called Front Street) are located. Since the law of Virginia at that time required that a judicial hanging be made public, it was expected that thousands of people would come to witness the execution. It was necessary, therefore, to select a site for the hanging at a place that would be convenient to reach and adequate in area to meet the requirements of the expected throngs of curious spectators.

The high sheriff believed there were places adequate for the event to be found both on the east and on the west of the town's boundaries. Judge Summers insisted, however, that the execution not take place on the north side of the Kanawha but on the south side despite the fact there were no bridges across the river there at that time. The sole regular daytime conveyance across the Kanawha at Charleston then was a horse-powered ferryboat. It is true there were some part-time ferries operating but those were not for the services of the general public. So, the request made by the judge was difficult to understand under the known circumstances, but his request was approved. It was not until quite some time after the execution that the reason for the judge's choice of location became known. Since it was commonly believed then that ghosts are afraid to cross bodies of water, Judge Summers wanted to be sure Turley's ghost would be stranded on the south side of the Kanawha and never have an opportunity to bother him.

The location of the gallows built for the hanging of Turley was near the mouth of Ferry Branch on the south

116

side of the Kanawha River and opposite the mouth of the Elk River. Since all of the ferries available would not be capable of transporting the expected hordes of people from the northern side of the river to the place of the hanging, the river was temporarily "bridged" with old salt boats. These boats, some of which were a hundred feet long and fifty feet wide, with flat bottoms, had been used to transport salt from the furnaces at Kanawha Salines a few miles above Charleston to markets down the Ohio River at Cincinnati and Louisville. By placing the boats end to end, then fastening them together and boarding them over, a pontoon bridge was built across the river from shore to shore.

Early in the morning of that fair September day in 1858 that had been chosen for the time of the execution of Pres Turley, people by the hundreds began to arrive and continued to come right up to the time of the hanging. They lined both sides of the streets from the old jailhouse on Virginia Street down Court to Front Street, thence down the roadway to what is now Goshorn Street and on to the bank of the river where the pontoon bridge began. While they waited, many of them talked and laughed with a great deal of joviality as though it were a holiday. When they saw Turley being brought from the jailhouse in an old farm wagon and slowly pass through the masses of people along the route to the pontoon bridge, a hushed silence fell over the spectators. Turley was seated on the coffin that would soon receive his lifeless body and around him sat a half-dozen armed guards. They were there more to protect Turley from a possible attack by some overwrought bystanders than to keep the prisoner in custody.

As the procession moved along, Turley sat there seemingly unperturbed and occasionally waved his hand and said good-bye to those he recognized along the street. Behind the wagon came a sea of people marching in the

117

death parade. While the solemn procession moved slowly on its way, the tolling of the courthouse bell rang out loud and clear and heightened the tension of the occasion.

When the procession arrived at the location of the execution, Turley was led from the wagon to the platform of the gallows. There he was joined by a minister who read a few verses from the Bible, then delivered a mournful prayer. Throughout the whole proceeding, Turley remained calm and seemingly had closed from his mind any thoughts about his impending fate. Then the high sheriff placed a black hood over Turley's head and a noose was quickly adjusted around his neck. When the sheriff pulled the plug that released the trap door in the platform of the gallows, Turley fell through the opening, and hung there lifeless. The body was taken down, put in the coffin and returned to his homeplace on Coal River.

From start to finish, it was a sad day for Judge Summers. Shortly thereafter, he declared he would never again permit himself to be in a similar situation where he would have to sentence a person to death. He resigned from his position as judge of the Virginia court system and returned to private law practice. In subsequent years he was known to serve on numerous occasions as a defense lawyer for impoverished persons and without any expectation of financial reward.

Gifts for Bennie

It was nearly dark as little Johnny Taylor was on the way back home from an afternoon of fishing in Turkey Trot Pond. As he walked along the narrow dusty road with his fishing pole in one hand, and a bait can in the other, he whistled as a means of driving away any fears he might have of the approaching darkness. As he was passing his Uncle Pete Elmore's house, he thought he heard a crying sound coming from the direction of the house. He stopped whistling and stood there a few moments to see if the crying sound was repeated, but none came. Since his Uncle Pete and Aunt Sarah Jane had no children, Johnny surmised the noise most likely had been made by a wildcat on the bluff back of the house, so he promptly resumed his journey homeward.

Sometimes while Johnny fished in Turkey Trot Pond, he wondered about his Uncle Pete and Aunt Sarah Jane. They just did not seem to act the same after their only child, Bennie, had died at birth. Although Johnny was only seven years old at the time, he still remembered quite well about Bennie's funeral.

As he recalled, it was very early one foggy morning that Bennie's father came walking up to their place with a small pine wood box in his arms. After talking briefly in low voices with Johnny's parents, Gus and Matilda, they all went to the family cemetery a short distance back of the Taylor house. A small grave had already been prepared there for the burial. While the pine wood box was being placed in the grave, Gus began to recite the Twenty-third Psalm from memory. When he had finished, all then said the Lord's Prayer in unison. As Johnny and his mother and his Uncle Pete slowly walked back toward the house, Gus took a shovel and filled in the grave.

Johnny had also observed that his uncle and aunt never went any place together. One of them always stayed at the house. Whether any problems had arisen between them after the loss of their baby, he did not know. As far as he could tell, they seemed to enjoy a normal relationship with each other. After a time Johnny found other things to occupy his mind and thought no more about it that day.

In time, other people of the community began to report they had heard strange noises while in the environs of the Elmore house. Some said it sounded like a child screaming while others believed it to be a wild animal in distress. As a result, rumors began to circulate that the Elmore house was haunted with the ghost of baby Bennie. Such tales continued to be told, off and on, for months but no one seemed to have any real evidence that a ghost was there except the occasional noises that were heard.

One afternoon while Gus and Johnny were back on the hill working in the cornfield, Matilda and four-year-old son, Sidney, remained at home. When a scratching noise was heard at the front door, Sidney ran and opened it. He was so shocked to see the odd creature standing there, he slammed the door shut and ran to his mother screaming that he had seen a "bad boy" outside. Matilda went to the front door, opened it slightly then quickly closed it again.

"O My Heavens!" she said in a hushed voice. Then looking at Sidney, she said: "It's time for your nap, young feller." Then taking him by the hand, she led him to his bedroom.

Sometime later when Sidney awakened from his nap,

he asked his mother about the strange-looking creature he had seen at the front door.

"You just dreamed about it, Sidney," she replied. "You didn't really see anything. It was only a dream."

Other people in the community began to report the sighting of an odd-looking creature darting about the shrubbery in the environs of the Elmore place. One man said that as he was passing the Elmore garden early one morning, he saw a stumpy grotesque form shuffle in behind some gooseberry bushes. He hurried to the spot where he had last seen it but found only a gaping hole in the paling garden fence through which it most likely had escaped. He looked all about the adjoining field but the weeds there were so tall and dense he was unable to determine where it had fled.

One day while Johnny and Sidney were passing the Elmore house on their way to Turkey Trot Pond, a huge flock of pigeons flew overhead. One pigeon apparently became disoriented and crashed through an attic window on the front side of the Elmore house. While the two boys stood there, they saw their Aunt Sarah Jane come running out into the front yard to see what had caused the noise. When Johnny pointed to the broken window and told her a pigeon had flown through it, she cried: "Oh! Oh!" then covered her mouth with her hands.

At that moment two men from a neighboring farm came riding past the Elmore house and stopped to see what was drawing the attention of Sarah Jane and the boys. While all were looking at the broken window, a small grotesque-looking creature came to the window with the pigeon in his hands. He placed it gently to one of his cheeks and then to the other in a loving and affectionate manner. On seeing Sarah Jane standing in the yard below, he held the pigeon out through the broken window toward her and cried:

"See, Mama, big bird!"

121

"My baby talked!" Sarah Jane exclaimed. "Did you hear him? My baby talked!"

Then realizing the danger of the situation, she cried out: "Stand back, Bennie, or you'll fall! Stand back!"

Suddenly the pigeon fluttered loose from the boy's hands and flew away. In his reaching out to try to retrieve it, he lost his balance and tumbled out the window. Sarah Jane rushed closer to the house and caught him in her arms. For several minutes she held him tightly and kissed him. Though visibly shaken and with tears coursing down her cheeks, she turned to face her nephews and the men on horseback. In a quavering voice she said:

"This is my son, Bennie. All I ask is that you find it in your hearts to be kind to him. Pete and I have tried to protect him but now we will need your help, too. Thank God, our long nightmare is over."

Soon the strange story of the hidden child became public knowledge throughout the community. At the time when Bennie was born, his arrival was so sudden there was no time, nor apparent need, to seek the aid of a doctor or a midwife. Moreover, the baby was so grotesquely deformed and ugly Pete and Sarah Jane did not want anyone else to see it. Since it appeared that it could live only a short time, they decided to announce it had died at birth and they would observe a mock funeral in private. Then when it did die, they could take the body out at night and place it in the cemetery plot where the mock burial had taken place. In that way they could avoid having to endure the shame and embarrassment of having such a grotesquely ugly child. Their friends, likewise, would, in this way, be shielded from the trauma that most assuredly would befall them once they had occasion to view its pitiful condition.

Pete then hurried over to the Taylor place to tell his sister, Matilda and her husband, Gus, about the plans they had made and to ask their assistance. He explained to them that the baby was a hunchback, had a severly misshapen head, a broad harelip, weighed no more than three pounds and could not possibly live more than a few days. What he and Sarah Jane wanted them to understand was their sincere feeling of compassion for all concerned.

For some time, Gus and Matilda argued that it was terribly wrong to do as they planned. No matter how deformed or ugly a baby was at birth, they said, its parents should not be ashamed of it; in that condition it needed, more than ever, an abundance of loving care. Eventually, Pete was able to get them to agree to keep mum about the plan and to permit the burial in the Taylor cemetery.

Despite Bennie's precarious health in his early infancy, he did not die as was expected. Sarah Jane kept him hidden in an attic room of their house month after month where she spent most of her time caring for him. Although he grew stronger physically, he was very slow in developing mentally. By the time he had reached the age of two and had never spoken a word, Sarah Jane began to spend hours with him trying to teach him to talk but he failed to respond. Sometimes she had a feeling her son had survived as a just punishment of her and Pete for hoping he would die soon after his birth.

Despite Bennie's appearance, Sarah Jane came to love him dearly. Many times she wished she could find an easy way to let the neighbors know about her child but in all of her thoughts about it, she could not envision a compassionate response from them. Then on those occasions when he got out of the house and ran into the garden and even, on one occasion, went to the Taylor place, she was worried sick over the possibility he might be harmed and, also, that her terrible secret might be found out.

123

A few weeks after Bennie's existence became known to the people of the community, they decided to have a little surprise party for him. On a quiet Sunday afternoon they began to drift in, a few at a time, to the Elmore place bearing gifts for Bennie. Soon the whole front yard was filled with people. When Pete and Sarah Jane finally came to understand the purpose of their coming, they were overcome with emotion.

There was laughter, and some tears, at Bennie's party that afternoon and all who came felt better for being there. Although Bennie received many gifts, they were only tokens of the greatest gift of all, the gift of acceptance by the people of the community.

About the Author

James Gay Jones was a native of West Virginia. He attended the public schools of Roane County, received an A.B. degree from Glenville State College and M.A. and Ph.D. degrees from West Virginia University.

His experience in the teaching profession has been in one-room rural schools, in high schools, an instructor of history at New York State University (Albany) and at West Virginia University. He was a professor of history and political science at Glenville State College, from which he retired in 1975.

In both his professional training and teaching experience, Dr. Jones had a major interest in local and regional history. While at Glenville State, he taught a course in West Virginia history over a period of twenty-five years during which time he learned of many of the tales that appear in his four books of folklore, namely *Appalachian Ghost Stories and Other Tales* (1975), *Haunted Valley and More Folk Tales of Appalachia* (1979), *A Wayfaring Sin-eater and Other Tales of Appalachia* (1983), and *More Appalachian Folk Tales* (1993).

Made in the USA
Monee, IL
07 July 2026